Home Workshop Prototype Firearms

How to Design, Build, and Sell Your Own Small Arms

Bill Holmes

Paladin Press • Boulder, Colorado

Other books by Bill Holmes:

Home Workshop Guns for Defense and Resistance:
    Volume I: The Submachine Gun

Home Workshop Guns for Defense and Resistance:
    Volume II: The Handgun

Home Workshop Prototype Firearms:
    How to Design, Build, and Sell Your Own Small Arms
by Bill Holmes

Copyright © 1994 by Bill Holmes

ISBN 0-87364-792-0
Printed in the United States of America

Published by Paladin Press, a division of
Paladin Enterprises, Inc., P.O. Box 1307,
Boulder, Colorado 80306, USA.
(303) 443-7250

Direct inquiries and/or orders to the above address.

Contents

Introduction

If the mail I get pertaining to the subject is any indication, there is widespread interest in designing and building firearms in one's own home or workshop. Unfortunately, far too many of these would-be gun builders lack a little something when it comes to designing a workable firearm, and even more when it comes to building it.

A prime example of this comes from a letter I received from a would-be gun builder who resides in a northwestern state, describing an automatic rifle which he said he intended to build. According to his letter, it would be a full-automatic rifle, chambered for the .50-caliber machine gun cartridge, made entirely from "C.R.S." (which I assume meant cold-rolled steel), and "straight blowback." He went on to say that the rifle would have a fiberglass stock and 20-round magazine and weigh 15 pounds, complete with telescopic sight.

Now this all sounds pretty good to the average person. However if put into practice, his plan would contain a number of design flaws. In the first place, "cold-rolled steel" is a common nickname for a low-carbon steel known as 1018. If this is the material my correspondent had in mind, it would be about as poor a choice there is to fabricate a firearm from. The reason for this is that 1018 simply will not heat-treat to the hardness required to prevent battering or upsetting and would wear rapidly. Also, this material does not have sufficient tensile strength or the ductility required to withstand the shocks and stresses imparted by heavy caliber firearms, or light calibers either for that matter. We will discuss this further in the chapter on materials.

Also, it should be noted that "straight blowback" is practical only in firearms chambered for low- or medium-pressure cartridges, mostly pistol cartridges of low to medium power. The reason for this is that the breech of such a gun is not locked at the moment of firing. Only the weight of the breechblock, or bolt, usually combined with forward pressure from one or more recoil springs, keeps the action closed at the instant of firing. Also, since the

1

pressure generated by the burning powder is exerted in all directions, it pushes the cartridge case walls outward against the chamber as well as pushes the head, or base portion of the case, to the rear against the breechblock and out of the chamber with the same amount of force applied to the base of the bullet to push it up the bore. Therefore, the bolt or breechblock must be of sufficient weight to remain closed until the bullet is well up or out of the bore and the pressure has diminished significantly. If it opens too soon, it will either pull the head off the cartridge case since the case walls grip the chamber wall, or it will blow the case apart. Either condition is extremely dangerous since it allows the hot gasses to escape from the breech end, sometimes accompanied by bits of metal from the blown-apart cartridge case. This not only may cause bodily harm to the user and anyone else close by, but it may blow the gun apart. In the case of the .50 caliber, this breechblock would have to weigh so much and would be so cumbersome that it would render such a firearm impractical.

Another widespread idea that doesn't quite work out the way people think it will is this business of "filing down the sear to make it a full automatic." Seldom does a week go by without my receiving a letter from some well-meaning soul with more mouth than brains describing in detail just how easy it is to do a full-automatic weapon conversion using this method. Here again, it doesn't work out in practice quite the way it does in theory.

What will happen here, in the event that a file will actually cut the hardened sear, is that when you do get it filed or ground or whatever, it doesn't hold the hammer or striker in the cocked position anymore. You are now required, after inserting a loaded magazine, to pull the slide or bolt to the rear and allow it to slam forward. At this time, if the firing pin is long enough to fire the chambered round (an inertia-type short firing pin probably won't do anything), the weapon will fire and keep on firing until it is empty or jams. There is no way to stop it. The trigger doesn't do anything anymore. Fortunately, most guns jam on about the second or third shot after being subjected to this modification., so not as many people get hurt as would be likely if this "conversion" worked the way it was supposed to.

Another expert told me last week how you could pull a toy balloon over the muzzle of a .22 barrel and shoot with absolute silence.

This book, then, is intended primarily to describe what actually will and what won't work in designing and building a prototype firearm and address the problems inherent in amateur firearms design. Most of what is contained in this book I know will work because I have tried it. Most of what won't work I also know about because I have tried that too.

Some of the material in this book is similar to parts included in some of my other books. I regret this in a way, but on the other hand, I cannot assume that everyone has all my other works, and I want this book to be as complete as possible. So bear with me if you find that you are reading something here that you have seen before. Someone else may be reading it for the first time.

A tremendous amount of work is required to design and build a firearm from raw material. Most of the time it is accompanied by quite a lot of frustration. Once it has been accomplished, however, and the finished working firearm is in hand, there is a feeling of pride and accomplishment that must surely be somewhat similar to what a mother feels when she looks on her newborn child for the first time. And since beauty is in the eye of the beholder, you and I could never build an ugly gun, no matter how it looks to others.

Chapter

Gaining Experience

1

How does one learn to build guns? This is the question most frequently asked.

Well there are gunsmithing schools, which may or may not teach you what you need to know. They probably will show you how to put together custom rifles and accurize pistols. But when it comes to actually designing and building a firearm from raw material, from what I have seen they are somewhat lacking.

Today there are people scattered throughout the country calling themselves "gunmakers," and probably not over a dozen have actually made a gun. One of these people recently moved into a nearby town. I met him at a gun show, where he had a couple of tables on which were displayed several rifles built on military Mauser actions with commercial barrels installed and a popular brand of "almost finished" stocks on them that he had fit and finished. He was passing out cards with his name and address on them along with the title "Gunmaker."

"Do you have any guns here that you actually made?" I asked.

"All of these," he said, sweeping his hand across the tables.

"No, no," I replied. "Not guns you simply assembled; guns that you actually made."

At this point, he admitted that this was what he called making a gun. He had never actually made a gun. He was just a mechanic.

My own experience started back around 1940. I was 12 years old at the time, but I was already into refinishing old guns and trying to make stocks. Back then, at least in our area, most centerfire rifles were lever actions. The .22s, were Remington and Winchester pumps, and the shotguns consisted mostly of double-barrels. Many of these had broken stocks, which I attempted to replace. I had a rasp, three or four chisels, a drawknife, and a hand drill. My dad had a workbench with a good heavy vise mounted on it, and a local blacksmith had a band saw. He sawed my stocks to shape form—or he did until one day

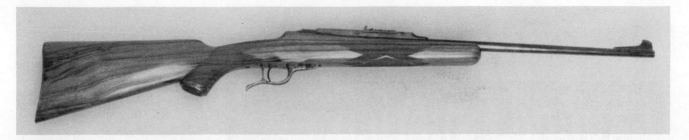

Holmes falling-block single-shot rifle.

Holmes 9mm autoloading pistol.

Holmes 9mm auto with 6- and 16-inch barrels and detachable buttstock. A pistol with a 6-inch barrel and a detachable stock requires a tax stamp and BATF registration (it's considered a "short-barreled rifle").

he sawed two of his fingers off. After that, I sawed them myself.

As I gained experience, the quality of my work improved, and it fell my lot to restock most of the guns with broken stocks in our community. By the time I was 14, I had already made over a hundred stocks, mostly for side-lock, double-barrel shotguns, and all from the block. There were no semifinished stocks for these guns.

Shortly after World War II started, we moved to California, where my parents both worked for Lockheed. This was the best thing that ever happened to me education wise. The high school I attended had a well-equipped metal shop as well as a wood shop—and, most important, an instructor who actually took a keen interest in anyone who really wanted to learn.

I became acquainted with most of the good gunsmiths in the area. Arthur Shivell, Powell and Miller of Pasadena (designers of the Powell Miller Venturied Freebore, or PMVF, cartridges, which were copied by Weatherby), and, most important of all, Joe Pfeifer. Joe had a clubfoot and wore a heavily built-up shoe to compensate for it. This kept him out of the military, and he had a shop in his garage in Roscoe, (later called Sun Valley) California. For some reason these people took an interest in me and showed me how to do most phases of gun work.

I bought a low-number Springfield action from Shivell that was supposedly reheat-treated by Sedgley and hit Joe Pfeifer up for a barrel blank. He said he didn't have any material to make one from, but if I could come up with a suitable piece of material, he would make me one. At the time, all suitable steel for such jobs went to the war effort.

About this time, we made a trip back to Arkansas, where I managed to come up with a Model T Ford truck drive shaft. I took this back to Joe, who seemed overjoyed to get it. It contained enough material for three barrels. He drilled and rifled one for me in exchange for the other two pieces.

With some help from the metal shop instructor, I turned it to what was considered a "sporter" contour and threaded it. I got a discarded military barrel from somewhere and copied the approach cone and extractor slot. Then I took it back to Joe, who chambered it for me. No chamber reamers were available at the time.

I tried to order a semi-inletted stock from both Stoeger and Bishop (they cost five dollars at that time), only to have my money returned. None were available for the duration of the war. Fortunately, one of my father's buddies came to my rescue. He had several walnut planks of sufficient thickness, which, he said, were in the attic of his house when he moved there several years before. He said he had no use for them, so he gave them to me. I made my own stock.

Holmes .22 autoloading pistol.

My first 12-gauge autoloading shotgun.

This was an experimental gun, built to see if it would silence a shotgun effectively. It still sounded as loud as a .38 Special, though it reduced recoil to almost nothing.

My second 12-gauge autoloader.

Holmes 12-gauge autoloading shotgun.

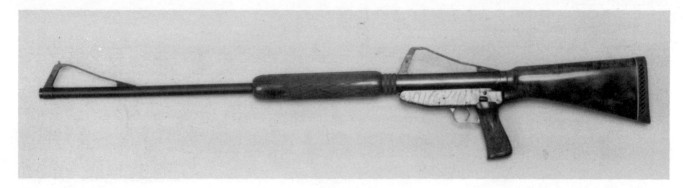

Holmes self-opening trap gun.

One of the gunsmiths I knew, I don't remember which one, gave me a Lyman 48 receiver sight and a ramp front sight, which I installed on the rifle. I really wanted a Weaver 330 or a Lyman Alaskan telescope sight, but none were available at a price I could afford.

We mixed a bluing solution in the school chemistry lab from a formula I got from one of the old gunsmithing books, and I polished the gun entirely by hand, using files, emery cloth, and sandpaper.

I now had what I thought was a pretty nice rifle, and I should have left it alone. But Clyde Baker's book talked about making checkering tools from umbrella ribs, and I had to try this. Needless to say, the addition of this checkering job did not improve the appearance of my rifle.

A little later on, Monte Kennedy and a couple of other people started a gun operation near where we lived. Naturally, I started going over

there to try to learn something new. In the course of our conversations, I let slip that I also made gunstocks. They immediately wanted to see one. I guess they thought it inconceivable that a 16-year-old kid could make a gunstock. I didn't much want to show them any since their guns were obviously superior to mine, but I took my rifle and a double-barrel shotgun over and showed them both guns.

To my surprise, they didn't laugh. "Hell, kid," Kennedy said, "these would be pretty good stocks if you hadn't fucked the checkering up." He proceeded to show me how to lay checkering out and gave me some good checkering tools. My checkering improved quite a bit after that.

Another man who helped me a lot was a vagrant blacksmith named Pete. I never heard his last name or knew where he came from. One day there was a Model T Ford truck parked on a

AR-15/M16 conversion with folding stock.

Latest version of my 12-gauge slide action shotgun. This one had a "camo" paint job, which didn't add anything to its appearance.

An experimental 9mm closed-bolt pistol.

A 9mm conversion unit on an AR-15/M16 lower receiver shown with a detachable butt stock; 16-, 10- (mounted), and 6-inch barrels; and 15- and 30-round magazines. Using an original M16 receiver to make a 6-inch-barrel pistol is making a "short-barreled rifle" according to the BATF.

Left side of a 12-gauge slide-action shotgun.

vacant lot just down the street from where we lived with a large tent erected beside it. These belonged to Pete. It turned out that the owner of the lot let Pete camp there in exchange for Pete's shoeing his horses. He not only took care of all the horses in the neighborhood but did whatever welding anyone needed. He sharpened tools, repaired automobiles, fixed home appliances, repaired watches and clocks, and, most important of all, worked on guns.

Pete didn't have much use for most of the kids in the neighborhood. They teased him and wouldn't leave his property alone. But he liked me, mostly, I suppose, because I treated him with respect and didn't touch anything that belonged to him without permission. I think this was probably the reason most of the area gunsmiths tolerated me. I know at least one of them kept all the others run off. But he was nice to me.

Pete showed me how to put case-hardening colors that looked better than the real thing on gun frames without a lot of heat. He showed me how to make parts from raw material with only a file, a hacksaw, and a hand drill. Even more important, he taught me how to heat-treat the finished part. He stayed camped there for several months, and finally one day he was gone. I was sorry to see him go.

After the war we moved to Cimarron, New Mexico, where my father owned and operated a sawmill. P.O. Ackley and George Turner started a gun making operation there called Ackley and Turner, which went bankrupt in short order. Ackley went on up to Trinidad, Colorado, and talked his way into a teaching position in a gunsmith school. Turner started a company to manufacture cattle squeeze chutes. He was the real brains behind their gun making business. He was taper boring shotgun barrels and cutting long forcing cones 50 years ago, long before these latter-day gunsmiths invented such things. I learned a lot from him too.

After a stint in the army, the last year of which was mostly spent sporterizing 03A4 rifles for the big brass, I went to Georgia. Here, among other things, I designed and built several specialty weapons for a government agency. I was also involved in refurbishing and modifying a number of weapons that went to Fidel Castro back before he ran Fulgencio Batista out and took over Cuba.

During this period, one of the leading gunsmiths in the area decided to start a gunsmith school. He seemed to think I should enroll in his school. I told him I didn't have time, but he stayed after me to try it for a few days just to see if I didn't need to attend. By the end of the second day, I realized that I already knew more than he did. I didn't go back.

In 1964, I had a series of disagreements with some of the people I was doing work for, so my family and I moved back to Arkansas. Here I intended to do gun repair and custom rifle and shotgun work. But it wasn't long before I was contacted by some of the people I had dealt with before wanting various special purpose guns, so I was right back into design and fabrication again.

I built an all-plastic .22 pistol that would pass through any metal detector in the world. It wasn't really all plastic; it was mostly nylon and had a ceramic firing pin. Ammunition for this weapon was concealed in a special belt buckle. Several were smuggled aboard aircraft completely undetected.

I built several intermediate-range sniper rifles. These were bolt actions, chambered for the .45 ACP cartridge, and used M1911 .45 pistol magazines. They were silencer equipped and capable of hitting quart oil cans consistently at 200 yards when properly sighted in.

I built several longer-range sniper rifles in both .308 and .300 Winchester Magnum. These were all-metal rifles with quick takedowns that could be contained in a 26-inch case. Calibers were interchangeable by switching barrels and boltheads. These rifles would hit quart oil cans consistently at 500 yards.

I also built .22 open-bolt machine guns that everyone said wouldn't work. They said the cartridge case would hang under the firing pin and jam the gun. I put the firing pin at the bottom and let the cartridge head slide across it, something no one had ever thought of before. Open-bolt guns, closed-bolt guns, locked-breech guns—I made them all at one time or another. I also built semiautomatic versions of these for the civilian market.

I built several versions of an autoloading box-magazine shotgun before I finally got one that suited me. I also built a slide-action version of this gun. Several companies contracted to produce them, but all they actually produced was wind.

I built trap guns with very little recoil and several versions of a single-shot falling-block rifle.

So, you see, I've acquired the experience, mostly the hard way. It took several years, but I learned.

I am sure you could learn a lot in a gunsmith school if you really wanted to, but it would mostly cover custom rifle work and the like. If you expect to actually design and manufacture firearms, your time will be better spent in a good vo-tech school learning to set up and operate precision machine tools. Then, with a few years of experience, you should be able to make anything you dream up. All by yourself. In your own shop.

Chapter
Tools and Equipment
2

While it is possible (although time consuming) to build a firearm in its entirety with a few files, a hand hacksaw, and a hand drill, decent power tools will not only cut down the construction time but probably also improve the quality of the finished work considerably. Let's take a look at some of the equipment that would be required for an operation of this kind.

Probably the most important item is an engine lathe. With suitable accessories and tooling, such a machine can perform all sorts of operations, including turning, threading, boring, and knurling. With a milling attachment, it can in many instances substitute for a milling machine, take the place of a drill press, and when properly equipped, even put rifling in barrels.

When contemplating the purchase of a lathe for the first time, far too many people actually go out of their way to seek out the smallest machine they can find, not only to save money but with the mistaken idea that the smaller machines are actually more precise when making small parts.

In fact, I read an article sometime back by a self-proclaimed lathe expert in which he stated that a small 6- to 9-inch lathe was best for making most gun parts. He claimed that a larger lathe of 14 to 16 inches would be clumsy to operate, and that the operator would probably break such small parts as firing pins when attempting to turn them on the larger machine.

As far as this writer is concerned, the truth of the matter is that a modern geared head lathe with a 14- or 15-inch swing and 40 inches or more between centers is the only way to go. Such a machine usually weighs a ton or more and, when properly set up on a rigid surface and leveled, will provide a solid, vibration-free platform for turning operations. The geared head machine, in addition to its ease in changing speeds compared to a belt-driven headstock, will also allow heavier cuts to be taken with less tendency to chatter than the belt-drive machine is capable of.

The machine should be level, both lengthwise and crosswise, and preferably bolted to the floor.

A 17-inch lathe, as shown here, is sturdy, accurate, and vibration-free. A 13-inch lathe is adequate and less expensive.

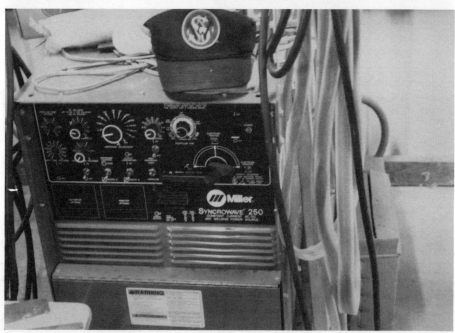

This welding machine will do MIG, TIG, and stick welding.

Many novices neglect to do this, and not only does accuracy suffer, but the machine may wear rapidly due to misalignment.

Most machines of this size will come equipped with three-phase motors. Unless three-phase power is available at your installation, you will require some sort of converter to allow running the motors on single-phase current. These are available through machine tool supply houses, ranging from small boxes for use with one motor to the large Rotophase types, which,

when properly wired into the circuit, will start and run a whole shop full of motors. These are also expensive.

Both a three-jaw and a four-jaw chuck should be acquired with the lathe if possible. If only one chuck can be afforded, it should be the four jaw since irregular shapes as well as round can be centered precisely through individual movement of the four jaws, whereas the three jaws open and close simultaneously and will only accommodate round stock.

A milling machine is almost mandatory if much work is anticipated.

Precise drilling operations can be simplified by using the mill as a drill press.

A set of collets and a collet closer would be nice to have, as well as a quick-change tool post, a live center for the tailstock, a drill chuck, a steady rest, a follower rest, and also, if possible, an adjustable automatic carriage stop.

To better understand why I suggest such extras as an automatic carriage stop, perhaps it would be worthwhile to describe my own shop and its operation.

My shop is a one-man shop. At present I am engaged in building a trap gun of my own design. By working long hours and running several machines at the same time, I can usually build three of these guns per month. I know, I could hire some help and probably up production. But I have tried it several times in the past, and after a while the employees decided that they knew more than I did and didn't need to do what I told them. I don't like to argue, so I work by myself. If it isn't right, there is only me to blame.

I have two engine lathes: a 15-inch Colchester

A metal-cutting saw is useful.

A "cold saw" is faster than a continuous-blade type.

and, parallel to it but facing the opposite direction with a 4-foot walkway in between, a 14-inch Taiwan-made lathe. At one end of the walkway stands an Induma vertical milling machine, while at the other end is a Bridgeport vertical mill. Each has a power feed on the table. Arranged in close proximity as they are, it is possible to run at least two and much of the time all four of these machines at the same time simply by setting up a cut and engaging the power feed of each. Since the automatic carriage stop

will disengage the power feed when it reaches the end of the cut, I can simply go from one machine to the next, setting up a new cut and restarting the power feed.

Located just a short distance away from these four machines, I have a small turret lathe, a combination MIG, TIG, and stick-welding machine, as well as an oxy/acetylene welding and cutting outfit. I have a horizontal metal-cutting band saw with an automatic shut off (which means I don't have to stand over it to shut it off when it

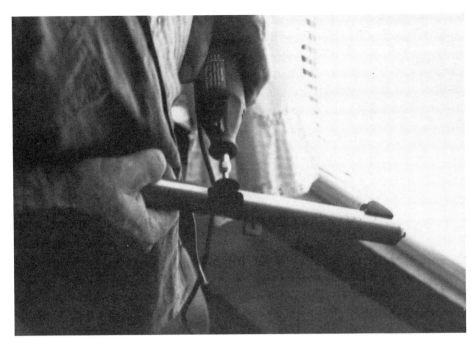

If no milling machine is available, slots and openings can be cut with a hand grinder using cut-off wheels.

finishes a cut), a wood-cutting band saw, and a large vertical metal-cutting band saw. This last machine is even more versatile because it has a built-in blade welder and grinder. This enables me to buy blade material in 100-foot rolls and make up blades for all three saws at a fraction of the cost of ready-made blades.

I also have a surface grinder, a small electric heat-treat furnace, a pedestal grinder, and a couple of bench grinders. Some polishing equipment coupled with a bluing setup and the usual files and hand tools pretty well round out the shop, giving me the capacity to make up about anything I might want in the firearms line. Now if I only had the skills and ability to go with the tools and machines . . .

You probably noticed that I did not mention owning a drill press. This is because I do not have a drill press as such. By mounting a drill chuck in the milling machine, I not only have a solid, sturdy drill press, but I can locate holes exactly where I want them without any guesswork.

The most versatile milling machine for our purpose is a full-size Bridgeport-type machine with at least a 42-inch table. If you anticipate installing ribs on shotgun barrels or machining rifle barrels to a cross section other than round, then a 48- or 49-inch table machine should be procured. Although most gun setups require only a mill vise and no more than four collets—specifically 1/4, 3/8, 1/2, and 3/4 inches—to take care of 90 percent of any work you may contemplate, it is desirable to have a full set of collets from 1/8 to 3/4 inch by sixteenths. A drill chuck is a required item. Also useful at times are a rotary table, a dividing head, and a boring head. As previously mentioned, a power feed on the machine will allow it to run while you perform other work and is almost like having an extra man in the shop, except you won't have to argue with him.

As with the lathe, the milling machine should be level both lengthwise and crosswise and bolted to the floor. Close attention should be paid to making sure the vise jaws are parallel to the table. Otherwise the machine will not make parallel cuts. I could have bought a little Clausing milling machine at just about my own price not long ago from a fellow who thought it was worn out. I aligned the vise with the table (it was cocked about 2 degrees), leveled the machine, and bolted it down for him. After we ran it for a little while, he took it off the market. He said it was like having a new machine and was no longer for sale.

Many experienced machinists neglect bolting the machines down. Some even snicker when it is suggested. While it is true that the weight of the machine usually will make it fairly solid, bolting it down will dampen and absorb vibration. This, to me at least, makes it worthwhile.

The welding equipment that you should own depends on what types of welding you are proficient at or willing to become proficient at. I say willing to become proficient because to become good at it you must practice, practice, and practice some more. This is the only way to become a first-class welder. You can learn how from books or schools, but experience is the only way to develop proficiency. If you are capable of using them, there are combination machines available that will do TIG (this stands for Tungsten Inert Gas) welding, which is often referred to as heli arc welding, MIG welding (this is a wire-feed process), as well as stick welding, which will take care of about any welding jobs you need to do.

Lacking the skill to use the welding equipment, the best alternative is to find a full-time welder who understands guns and will realize that beads must be built up above the surface to permit machining flush, and what effect polishing and bluing will have on it. The average heavy equipment welder who spends his time welding on bulldozers, dump trucks, and the like will usually ruin the kind of work you need him to do and should generally be avoided.

In any event, the shop should have an oxy/acetylene outfit to be used for silver soldering, brazing, welding, and cutting, and to apply heat for certain bending and forging operations. It can also be used to harden and temper certain types of steel when no furnace is available.

You will also need a grinder of some sort. A good vise is essential, as is a metal-cutting band saw. Such saws are available for both horizontal and vertical use. Use it horizontally to cut material to length. Vertically it can be used to saw parts such as hammers, triggers, and sears almost to shape, after which they can be finished by milling, grinding, or filing.

Several files of assorted shapes and sizes should be on hand, together with a few metal-cutting chisels, some punches, a scriber or two, and a square and level. Other items can be acquired as needed.

Chapter

Materials

3

Quality firearms should be made of wood and steel. At times it is acceptable to use aluminum as a weight-saving measure. Shotgun muzzle brake bodies are an example of this. But, what I refer to as "pot metal" such as zinc, zamak, pewter, and the like should be avoided.

Quality sporting firearms will have stocks made from high-quality hardwood such as walnut, maple, or myrtle. Beech, gum, sycamore, and the like are used on cheaper guns and are, at most, second best.

There has been a trend over the past several years to try and brainwash the shooting public as to the superiority of synthetic stocks for use on hunting rifles and shotguns. This is mostly a pipe dream that the manufacturers have conned the gun writers into believing and passing on.

While it may be true that in some instances these are more stable and less apt to warp than their wood counterparts (try leaving one out in the hot sun all day), and they are supposedly less prone to cracking and breaking (try drop-ping one on a hard surface in cold weather), the real advantage is the cost saving due to cheaper materials and less labor.

I have used synthetic stocks and forends myself in the fabrication of military-type weapons and, at one time, in an economy-grade trap gun that I intended to market. This was done, in the case of the military weapons, primarily to save weight, but also because I could obtain surplus M16 stocks at extremely low prices (from $2 to $8 dollars each) and easily adapt them to fit my guns. In the case of the trap gun, I molded the grip, used modified M16 butt-stocks, and turned the forend from black nylon. The time saved in finishing and elimination of checkering, plus cheaper materials (I used wood costing $200 in the deluxe-grade gun, as opposed to $15 worth of materials in the economy grade), was passed on to the customer in the lower-priced gun.

There are all sorts of cheaper grades of steel that could be used to fabricate the metal parts, that is, if we only intended to fire a few rounds through the gun. But what we are seeking here are materials to make our parts that will last for several thousand rounds and more. Therefore, we must seek out and set in place the best materials available for this purpose. While there are people who would question my choices, as far as I am concerned, chrome molybdenum steels such as 4130, 4140, and 4150 are suitable to build the entire gun. Known as Chrome moly, Brake die, Maxell and other nicknames, these steels are easily heat treated, machine cleanly, and possess high tensile strength and elasticity. Furthermore they can be welded without ruining them, as sometimes occurs with other steels.

Nickel steels of the 2330-2340 variety are also entirely usable, as are the nickel chromium steels designated 3130, 3135, or 3140.

The numbers associated with these steels, in case anyone is wondering, are partial descriptions of their compositions. The first figure describes the class to which the steel belongs. The second figure indicates the percentage of the main alloying element. The last two figures indicate the carbon content in hundredths of one percent or "points." Therefore, 3140, as an example, describes a nickel steel with approximately 1 percent nickel content and a carbon content of forty hundredths of one percent, sometimes referred to as 40 points of carbon.

4130 seamless tubing is ideal for shotgun barrels, tubular receivers, and the like. It is usually available from metal supply houses in so many inside diameters and wall thicknesses that at least one will be close enough to adapt to your use.

Round stock is available in the desired compositions and in almost any diameter needed from these same metal supply houses. Flat stock for hammers, sears, triggers, etc., is also available from the same sources in almost any fractional thickness desired.

In many cases, these materials must be purchased in rather large quantities. If the vendor can be persuaded to cut off the small quantity desired, they will charge you an exorbitant price for it. Many metal supply companies will try to charge $15 to $25 just to saw a piece of metal in two.

Therefore, when only one gun is to be built, look for some other source of materials. Automobile and truck axles contain material suitable for bolts, barrel extensions, gas cylinders, and whatever other round parts are need-

ed. Actually, if sawed into strips, flat parts can also be made. Axles can usually be obtained from salvage yards for $2 to $5 dollars each. Leaf springs, as used on the rear axles of older cars and pickup trucks as well as on larger trucks, are a source of flat stock. Hydraulic cylinders and discarded shock absorbers contain smaller-diameter shafts useful as round stock and tubing. This tubing will seldom, if ever, be adaptable to shotgun barrel use, but in certain instances it can be used for receivers. Motorcycle front forks will yield just about the same sizes and types of tubing and round stock as the hydraulic cylinders, as will large-diameter aluminum tubing, which can sometimes be used to make shotgun muzzle brake bodies.

Some of the material suggested, especially the axles and leaf springs, will be too hard to machine easily. They will require softening, or annealing. This is accomplished by heating the metal slightly above its critical point and allowing it to cool slowly. Since the average heat-treat furnace is too small to fit the axles or spring leaves, another method must be found.

Fire departments usually take a dim view of uncontained open fires within city limits, so you will likely have to go to the country to do this. Accumulate and pile up enough wood to make a fire that will completely surround the metal objects and burn for three or four hours. Place the metal objects on top of your wood pile and start it on fire. If you have enough wood, it will heat the metal to the required temperature. As the fire burns down, the metal parts will sink into the ashes, where they cool very slowly. They are usually left overnight; when removed the next morning, they will probably still be warm. They will also be softened to a point where they will machine easily.

The axles described are usually made from material with a high enough carbon content to permit heat treatment to any hardness desired. Many of these are made from the same 4140 recommended in the first place. They are also found made from 4150, 4340, 2340, 3140, and other alloys.

Leaf springs are mostly made from material with a high carbon content. Compositions commonly found in these are 1085, 1095, 4063, and 4067.

It should also be mentioned that the stems of

automobile engine valves are suitable for firing pins. They, too, must be annealed before they will machine freely.

After the component parts are cut to shape, fitted, and finished, they should be heat treated as detailed in Chapter 20. Properly done, parts made and heat treated as described will last a lifetime.

For those who think a gun should be made from stainless steel (I am not one of these), it should be noted here that seamless tubing of the same dimensions deemed proper for the shotgun barrels described is available with a cold-drawn finish in 416 stainless according to the company I buy from. Round and flat stock is available from the same source. If you must have stainless, an alloy called 416F, which is a nickel-bearing chromium steel with enough sulphur added to make it machine freely, is probably the best choice available.

There are any number of companies and individuals advertising gunstock wood in several of the gun magazines. If you will be satisfied with black walnut, a local lumber yard usually will have at least a small supply on hand. This is true in the eastern and midwestern states. In California and other far western states, one can also find a goodly supply of so called "English" and "Claro" walnut. It is advantageous to be able to examine wood before you buy it.

Most large cities have at least one plastic supply house that carries, or can get, black nylon or other synthetic material to use in forends. Fiberglass and epoxy can be found at auto parts houses. They sell it to body shops for use in auto body repair. Boat builders and repair shops also keep a supply on hand. If M16 buttstocks are required, several surplus gun parts suppliers advertise them for sale.

Chapter

What to Design

4

With an equipped shop in place, the next item on the agenda is to decide what to design and build.

Probably just as important is the question of what *not* to design. Of course, the opinions expressed here are my own, but with almost 50 years of experience and observation to draw on, I must be partly right.

There is no point in developing a firearm that even comes close to duplicating or replicating an existing design. Even if successful, it would only get a share of the market while competing with its predecessors. Unless obviously superior in one or more aspects, it probably will get less than a full share.

The Colt M1911 pistol is a good example of this. For several decades, the Colt and various foreign licensees stood alone (or almost alone) in their field without serious competition. Suddenly, after the patents expired, everybody and his brother tried to build a similar gun. In time, each got a little share of a market that had previously been dominated by the one maker. Most of these companies have fallen by the wayside, leaving only two or three who, as of this writing, are also in financial trouble.

Today, the high-capacity semiautomatic pistol is the only kind most shooters want to talk about. But there are already so many of these on the market that, unless one could come up with a design obviously superior to the rest, there is no point in trying to design another.

If one were to attempt another of these, probably the most noteworthy deviation from existing designs would be one with a fixed barrel and a separate bolt locking into the frame. This could very well result in a gun with superior accuracy, since the position of the barrel in relation to the sights would remain constant, or nearly so. There is also room for improvement in the triggers of these guns, especially in the double-action mode.

Actually, any design effort put forth probably should be devoted to developing some sort of manually operated action. Whether we like it or not, sooner or later the wrong person is going to

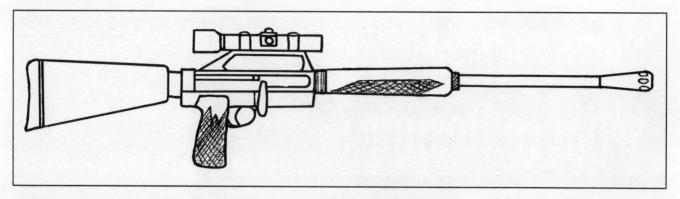

A rifle with a design such as this would have far less recoil than conventional designs.

This prototype 9mm autoloading pistol is being built as an improvement (?) over my original MP83. It also has a folded sheet metal lower receiver and sights made in the same manner. This gun has a longer receiver, allowing a longer, heavier bolt to be used, which slows down the cyclic rate. Both open- and closed-bolt models can be built by changing bolt and trigger assemblies. This one is also easier to build than my original gun. Both are made from wood and steel, not cheap plastic and pot metal.

This is an unfinished prototype autoloading .22 pistol designed to ease manufacture and correct shortcomings inherent in my original MP22. This gun has but one threaded union, which is at the muzzle end of the barrel, compared to three in the original. The lower receiver is folded from sheet metal instead of machined from aluminum, as was the other. The sights are also folded from sheet metal. Both open- and closed-bolt configurations are possible simply by changing bolts. When finished, this gun will have the forward portion of the upper receiver, which surrounds the barrel, ventilated with four rows of holes. Quite a bit of fabrication time can be saved building this gun as compared to the original.

get shot with a semiautomatic firearm. This will result in the law severely restricting or forbidding any more weapons of this type from being manufactured. Never mind the fact that these won't kill anyone any deader than any other gun. The so called "media," most of whom don't even know which end of a gun to load, are determined to bad mouth these guns. Sad to say, more and more people are succumbing to the influence of these antigun people. Even though the Second Amendment of the Constitution of the United States guarantees my and your right to bear arms uninfringed, there is a very good chance it will happen. So, anyone devoting enough effort to design and build a gun from now on with the intention of being able to market it should probably avoid automatic weapons of any sort.

In time, slide actions, or "pumps," will proba-

bly achieve popularity. These fire almost as fast as autoloaders and are far more likely to remain legal. There are people who will tell you that a slide action is more reliable than an autoloader due to the fact that "if it jams you can simply work the slide, thereby clearing the jam." This is not necessarily true. Most jams of this type that I've ever experienced required digging or prying the jammed round out of the gun the same way you would with the autoloader.

Shooters are becoming increasingly recoil conscious. Designs that lessen felt recoil significantly will gain popularity in the future. Shotgun recoil can be reduced greatly through use of the muzzle brake design shown in Chapter 11. Combined with an overbored or "backbored" barrel while incorporating a spring-loaded telescoping buttstock in a design that features a straight-line recoil and high sight line will result in a gun with almost no recoil. Note that I said almost. The only way I have found to make a gun "absolutely recoilless" as some have advertised is to leave the firing pin out. If it won't shoot, it can't kick.

Rifles can be designed in the same manner, except the oversize bore cannot be incorporated.

Bolt-action rifles have long been considered the ultimate accuracy wise. I have no quarrel with this. However, one designed and built incorporating the features described above, while not as attractive as the "classic" style rifle so popular with custom gun makers, will have much less felt recoil, especially in heavy calibers.

Single-shot falling-block actions have limited popularity, especially in rifles. There has been

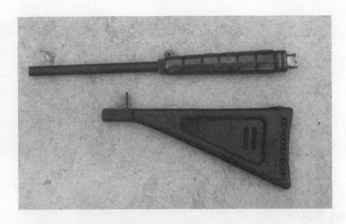

Interchangable barrels and detachable buttstocks, making a rifle and pistol combination, can be desirable features. However, if the short barrel is in place when the buttstock is added, an illegal weapon will result.

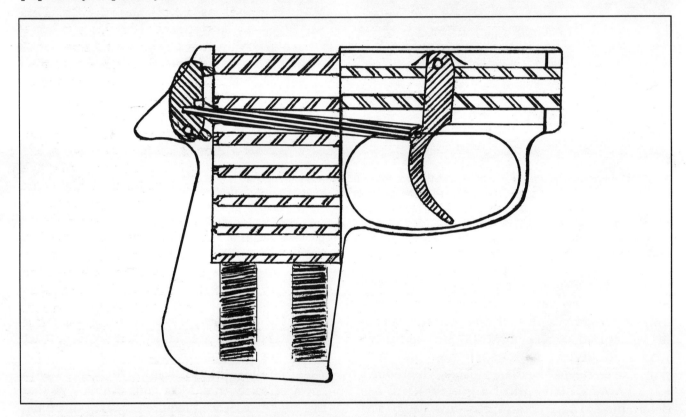

Rising-chamber compact pistol. A compact .22WRM is considered by many to be desirable for a "backup" or "hideaway" gun. One fault with this design would be the chamber block interfering with the sight line. However, since such a gun would be used at very short range, its compact size would outweigh this drawback. The trigger would be double-action only. By increasing the size slightly, larger calibers could be used.

Easy access to working parts is a desirable feature.

The result of inexperience, ignorance, and reloaded shells.

little significant change in the design of these in over a hundred years except to substitute coil springs for the leaf springs used in the originals. I built a few with two-piece receivers that were inletted into one-piece stocks in the same manner as a bolt-action rifle. This allowed a stock shape similar to the classic bolt-action design, and a number of people considered them quite attractive. There did not seem to be enough demand to justify the tooling costs required to mass produce them, and the shop-made guns cost too much to build, so they more or less fell by the wayside.

I have long thought that a high-grade top-break revolver built on the same principle as some of the older Smith and Wessons or maybe the British Webleys and Enfields would find a ready market. The speed and ease of ejecting empty cartridges combined with unimpeded access to the cylinder for reloading would offset any disadvantages inherent in the design. If properly designed, this should find a good market among combat revolver shooters.

The designer should always try to utilize preformed materials in a design as much as possible. In many cases, it is possible to use seamless tubing for receiver material that is already of a usable inside and outside diameter and already has a smooth finish, both inside and out. Shotgun barrels can be made from 4130 seamless tubing requiring very little finish work on the bore. It is also possible to obtain square or rectangular tubing that can be adapted to use as trigger housings, lower receivers, magazine housings, etc.

All dimensions should be kept to a standard size (fractional if possible). This will allow using standard-size round, square, and flat stock in many instances with very little machine work required to cut them to size. Saving manufacturing time and materials which will be reflected in lower production costs.

As far as I am concerned, firearms should be made from wood and steel where practical. Pot metal and plastic should be confined to BB guns and cap pistols; real guns should be built from quality materials. There are, of course, exceptions to this. Many military-type firearms require fiberglass or plastic stocks. In certain instances, aluminum can be substituted for steel to save weight (the shotgun muzzle brake described in this book is a good example of this). But for guns intended for civilian or sporting use, where quality should be your first consideration, such practices should be avoided when possible.

Chapter

Design Theory

5

As stated in an earlier chapter, firearms with high-capacity detachable box magazines, whether they be shotgun, rifle, or pistol, are becoming more desirable. These and specialty single shots such as trap guns and falling-block rifles seem like the logical types of firearms to develop.

Apart from the low-powered autoloading blowback actions, all firearms must be built around a locking system of sufficient strength to contain whatever pressure is generated during firing. These locking systems can consist of a rising or tipping block that locks the bolt body into the roof of the action, usually mating with a barrel extension; a rotating bolt, or bolthead in which lugs on the bolt rotate into recesses in the receiver, thereby locking the action; roller and inertia-locked actions and falling-block single shots, in which the breech block slides vertically, exposing and closing the chamber; as well as break actions.

It is my own opinion that autoloading firearm designs should be avoided. Sooner or later,

even more laws restricting their ownership and use will come into being, which will limit the market severely. If you should decide to pursue an autoloading or automatic design, every precaution should be taken to make it as difficult as possible to convert it to full automatic. Eventually, some bright lad will manage to turn one into a machine gun, assuming your gun is put into production, and then guess who will be in trouble.

I built and marketed such a gun at one time. Due to the design, it was necessary to put a projecting pin in one side of the sear, which acted as a disconnector. The trigger assembly could not be assembled with this pin in place. I reamed a tapered hole in the sear and, after final assembly, drove the pin in and bradded it on the back side. It never occurred to me that anyone would drive it out again. Removing this pin turned the gun into a full automatic. As long as the trigger was held back, the gun would continue to fire until empty. Of course it wouldn't fire single rounds anymore, which rendered it worthless as far as I am concerned. I like to hit targets with one shot instead of simply spraying bullets in the general direction of the target. But for some reason there are any number of people who get enjoyment out of spraying lead. The feds caught some people with converted guns, declared them all machine guns, and put an end to my pistol business.

The sad part is that with just a little more thought, the gun could have been made slightly different so that it would not have fired unless the pin was in place. It simply never entered my mind.

You should first define the intended use of the finished gun. This will, in many cases, determine barrel length, magazine capacity, caliber, and overall configuration. The action type can then be chosen.

For a number of years I have been fascinated by shotguns, both single-shot trap guns and high-capacity box magazine guns. So if I seem prejudiced toward these guns, bear with me. The same designs can be scaled up or down to fire rifle or pistol cartridges.

A magazine must be designed and built that will feed the specific cartridge or shell used. This should be done first and the gun designed around it, since a close-fitting magazine housing is desirable for foolproof feeding.

I learned the hard way that high-capacity shotgun magazines must have a curve to present the top shell in the same plane, regardless of how many shells the magazine has in it. Due to the rim, the shotgun shell is bigger at the back than at the front. A straight-bodied magazine will feed five, sometimes six shells fairly satisfactorily. But if more are added, the nose of the top shell dips to a point where it will no longer feed.

To determine the correct curve to cause each shell to feed on the proper plane, arrange a full load of shells atop each other, with each top rim just ahead of the one under it, on a piece of paper and draw a line along both the back and front. No computer is required to determine this, just common sense.

Magazines for rifle and pistol cartridges can usually be made in a straight-bodied double-row configuration. These cartridges are far easier to make feed from a magazine than are shotgun shells. In an ideal situation, the magazine lips will release the rear end of the shell or cartridge just as the nose of the round enters the chamber. This requires careful layout of the position of the magazine well in relation to the breech end of the barrel. Ejection should occur as soon as the empty case completely exits the chamber. This can be adjusted to compensate for any error in design calculation by making the ejector longer than required. and cutting it back to the proper length after the gun is finished.

Ejection ports must be of ample size to allow the empty case (or loaded round) to exit freely without interference. Especially in the case of the shotgun, the empty case must be ejected before the top round in the magazine pops up into feeding position. This requires the magazine to be positioned somewhat further to the rear, whereby the empty case is ejected while the bolt is still on top of the next round, keeping it out of contact with the empty case. The bolt must then travel further to the rear, allowing the next round to pop up into feeding position in front of the bolt face, which pushes it forward out of the magazine as the bolt closes.

Dependable feeding of rifle and pistol cartridges can usually be established by using an approach cone of some 40 to 45 degrees at the breech end of the barrel. Such a feeding system was incorporated into the design of the M1903 Springfield rifle as well as the M54 and pre-1964 M70 Winchester rifles, among others. This breeching system was frowned on and considered unsafe by writers and armchair experts for several years. Now it has been "rediscovered" by several producers of higher-grade guns.

The shotgun will require a feed ramp just in front of the magazine to guide the blunt-ended case upward into the chamber. The barrel extension will have an approach cone similar to that described for the rifle and pistol, except it will require a shallower angle.

A locking system must now be decided on. Probably the easiest system to make up in a small shop is one with a rotating bolthead (or a rotating bolt if bolt action is used) locking into a barrel extension. The barrel is threaded into the barrel extension, forming a solid unit whereby the bolt and barrel assembly are locked together. This can save a considerable amount of machining time and effort over cutting bolt locking recesses directly into the receiver, and it relieves the receiver of most stress and stretching action that would take place with the bolt locking directly into the receiver body.

The means of opening and closing the action must be chosen. If the bolt action is used, it will be little different to other bolt actions in principle. The number of locking lugs will determine the amount of bolt lift required. In a slide-action or autoloading design, the operating mechanism can encircle the barrel instead of hanging down under it as in existing designs. This will usually mean that only one action bar, which connects the operating mechanism to the bolt, can be used. However the action bars can be wider than normal and have curved cross sections, making them stiffer than the thin, flat action bars used in other designs. The autoloader would have the gas piston encircling the barrel, with the gas port(s) at a point close enough to the chamber to cause unlocking while there is still enough pressure in the barrel to give the bolt sufficient impetus to assure that it opens completely. This is especially important with the shotgun.

With the box-magazine gun, upward pressure from the magazine spring pushes the shells up against the lower side of the bolt, creating friction that is not present in a tubular-magazine gun. If any of the recoil-reduction devices, which includes the overbored barrel, are included in the design, the bolt will need all the help it can get to open completely. Even the tube-magazine guns already in existence sometimes fail to eject and feed when fired from the hip with the butt unsupported. This is another argument for the slide action.

The receiver must be long enough to contain the barrel extension at the forward end, plus the full length of the bolt, and be of sufficient length to allow the bolt to open completely. It must also be of sufficient diameter or width to allow the full width of the magazine to fit into the lower side, plus accommodate a full-sized ejection port just above it.

The bolt must be long enough so that in the closed and locked position, it extends far enough past the rear of the magazine opening for the firing mechanism—whether it be hammer fired, striker fired, or whatever—to mate with the parts in the lower receiver. If it is to be a hammer-fired gun, the only accommodation for the firing mechanism will be a lengthwise hole for the firing pin. If striker fired, not only a firing pin hole but a slot for the sear and a bored-out recess for a retainer bushing will be needed. If it's a turn bolt, a cocking cam must also be cut.

With a shotgun and most .22 rimfires, two extractors are required. Actually the outside one on the same side as the ejection port is the extractor. The inside one, just across from it, simply serves to hold the shell head in place against the bolt face during extraction. In rimless rifle and pistol cartridges, a counterbore in the bolt face serves to hold it in place.

Some sort of trigger housing or lower receiver must be used to house the firing mechanism. This will include a trigger guard, safety, and a means to mount the grip. The ejector is also fastened to this in some way, as is, in most cases, the magazine latch. While it is possible, and involves less work, to drill through both sides of the lower receiver for the hammer, sear, and trigger pivot pins, it is worthwhile to make up a separate housing to contain these parts and mount it inside the frame. This not only eliminates exposed pin or screw heads, which don't improve the appearance of the gun, but also prevents pins from working out, which can render the weapon inoperative.

Provision should be made for the buttstock to be attached to this assembly. This is usually accomplished through means of a drawbolt that extends through the buttstock and is threaded into the receiver.

Though a safety can be placed in several locations, one of the handiest is on the bottom side of the receiver directly forward of the trigger. Not only is it equally accessible to either hand, but it can be pushed forward into the firing position with the trigger finger. This was once the position favored by the military, but they got involved with incorporation of a selective-fire switch with the safety and moved it to the side of the gun, where it is easily accessible only to the right-handed shooter.

I made some shotguns once using an M16 hammer and trigger with the safety in the same position as the M16 selector switch/safety. About half the people interested in these guns were left-handed, so I wound up putting a safety lever on both sides so that it could be operated with either hand. This was similar to the ambidextrous safeties used on combat-type autoloading pistols. This safety worked fine, but it was complicated and difficult to make. The simple sliding safety just in front of the trigger corrected that.

A safety should be just that—a safety, rendering the gun incapable of discharging when it is engaged. This means it should lock the sear directly into the hammer notch, making accidental discharge impossible. Simply wedging the trigger in its forward position is not good enough. It is possible for the hammer to jar off the sear if dropped, especially if the hammer notch or sear nose angle is steeper than it should be. The safety shown in the shotgun drawings will pass any military drop test ever devised.

It is likewise imperative that a disconnector be devised to cam the trigger out of engagement so that the gun cannot fire until the action is locked. Properly fitted, when the bolt body is moved to the rear one eighth inch or more, the trigger is disconnected and the gun will not fire. Do not neglect this. I built a trap gun once with a straight pull bolt. It would have required a complicated arrangement to incorporate such a disconnector, so I left it out. I took this gun to a trap shoot and let several shooters try it. It didn't kick much and shot slightly high, so everybody liked it.

Everything went fine until I went into the club house to have a drink with the club manager. While we were in there, I heard a loud report. Sure enough, one of the "expert reloaders" had put a shell in the gun that wasn't resized properly, and it wouldn't let the bolt close enough to lock. It fired without being locked and blew the bolt to the rear. No trace of the empty case was found; it was simply blown to bits. No one was hurt, and neither was my gun. But if someone had been standing close to the ejection port, they could have been. I have never built another such gun without a proper disconnector.

A turnbolt action, in which the firing pin is cammed to the rear as the bolt is opened, will not need such a disconnector. While the firing pin will move forward if the trigger is pulled with the bolt partly open, the sear will contact the cocking cam, which will not allow the firing pin to travel forward far enough to contact the primer unless the bolt is almost completely closed.

If the slide-action gun is built, some means should be provided to keep the slide locked forward until either the trigger is pulled, causing it to be released, or a manual slide-release button is depressed. This will prevent the slide from jarring or vibrating partway open, which might

cause the trigger to disconnect and not fire when it is needed.

Regardless of the design or configuration, the sight line will be between 2 and 2 1/2 inches above the comb for comfortable shooting. This will fit the average shooter fairly well. Fat boys with thick cheeks will require slightly more. A length of pull (the distance from the buttplate to the trigger) of 13 1/2 to 14 inches will fit the average person. In a trap gun, where the weapon is shouldered and in the firing position when the target is called for, it can be somewhat longer. If the pistol grip design is used, the stock length is of less importance than with the standard stock. The forend should be long enough to prevent the shooter's hand from coming in contact with the hot barrel.

If the shotgun muzzle brake is used, the front sight should be mounted on top of it. It should have vertical adjustment incorporated into it so the shooter can move the point of impact in relation to the sight picture. Windage, or lateral pattern movement, is accomplished by rotating the muzzle brake slightly and locking it in place with the lock nut. In the trap gun especially, the rear aiming point should also have vertical adjustment, which will allow the shooter to move it up or down until it fits him exactly. This will eliminate one of his excuses for missing targets.

Most of the previous observations are also valid when applied to other designs. The single-shot falling-block action, while difficult to build, makes up into a most attractive firearm. If the receiver is built in two parts and inletted into a one-piece stock, it not only should be as accurate as a comparable bolt action, it also permits cleaner stock lines as found in the so called "classic" style custom rifles.

One of the most difficult tasks in building a falling-block gun is properly locating the spot for the firing pin hole. This can be made easier by turning a sharp point on a rod that will slip fit into the bore. The rod is inserted in the barrel with the pointed end toward the breech. With the breechblock closed and in firing position, the end of the rod extending from the muzzle is tapped with a hammer. The sharp point will mark the firing pin location.

If you are using a rimfire caliber, it is a simple matter to measure from the center mark the correct distance for the firing pin location. We read about people trying to locate rimfire firing pin locations by painting the head of a fired case with some sort of marking compound and closing the bolt on it. They say the firing pin depression won't leave any mark, and this locates where the firing pin is supposed to go. In practice, if the breechblock fits up snug against the breech end of the barrel as it should, whatever marking compound was painted on the head of the case will be smeared across the face of the breech block as it is closed and will therefore indicate nothing. Provision must also be made for the firing pin tip to retract before, or just as, the breechblock begins to open. Otherwise the firing pin will likely hang up in the fired primer or rim indentation and either break the firing pin or cause the action to be extremely hard to open.

When you have your design firmly fixed in your mind as to how you want it to look and work, it should be drawn, full size, on paper.

It is sometimes helpful to make cardboard cutouts of the working parts and pin them in place on the drawing. Many times little things like moving a pivot pin slightly or determining the correct location for a hammer notch can be accomplished through use of this method.

With the design finalized, it may be helpful to make up a full-scale model from wood, or plastic, or both. When the model is built, all sorts of little things that don't show up on drawings which can cause problems often become apparent. While this may seem like a lot of extra work, it is far better to discover miscalculations and design flaws and correct them on such a mockup than to discover them after the final project is mostly finished and maybe having to scrap part or all of it.

Chapter

Helpful Hints

6

The purpose of this chapter is to pass on any bit of information that I can think of which might be helpful to you. Some of it might have been included in other chapters. Other parts of it probably have no relevance whatsoever. But again, some of it might come in handy.

When drilling holes, if they are expected to be round and straight, sharp drills must be used. The material to be drilled should be clamped or held in a vise and secured to the mill or drill table. If you try to hold it in one hand and feed the drill into it with the other, as many people try to do, torque caused by resistance to the drill tries to turn the material in the opposite direction, causing the drill to crawl off center. This is the cause of most crooked or oversize holes.

Holes should be started, especially on rounded surfaces, with a center drill, drilled to depth with an undersize drill, and finished with a drill of the proper size. When holes are to be tapped partway through, the hole is first drilled with the tap drill, the full-size portion drilled for

clearance, and the hole tapped, in that order. When drilling for pivot pins, such as for a trigger or hammer, the frame or housing that the pivoting part fits into should be drilled from the side that the pin is installed from with a drill of the same size as the pin. The opposite side is drilled with a slightly smaller drill to grip the pin and hold it in place, and the hole through the pivoting part slightly larger so that it will pivot without binding.

Contrary to popular opinion, a .125-inch pin will not rotate freely in a .125-inch hole. Assuming that we are using a 1/8-inch pivot pin, we drill the hole completely through all surfaces with a No. 31 drill, which measures .120 inch, or .005 undersize. The one side is drilled to 1/8 inch, or .125 inch. The hole through the pivoting part is drilled with a 3.20 millimeter drill, which has a diameter of .126 inch. This will allow the part to pivot on the pin without resistance and still not wobble. Holes for other sized pins are done in the same manner.

Straight holes can be drilled fairly close to

their required location with a hand drill, provided that the work is clamped or otherwise secured to prevent its movement. Both hands should be used to hold the drill in an absolutely vertical position, or at 90 degrees to the work. Holes should be started with a center drill and drilled to depth with an undersize drill, followed by the drill of the correct size.

If absolute precision of hole location is essential, the milling machine should be used in the same manner as a drill press, with the work fastened securely to the table and moved into exact location with the table feeds. Even now, the center drill should be used first, followed by drills as described above.

Bolt lugs, raceways, holes spaced around the diameter, etc. are located and spaced through use of a rotary table, dividing head, or spacer. In the event none of these are available when needed, fair success can be had in locating equally spaced positions around the outside diameter by wrapping a strip of masking tape around the work and marking the exact length of one turn. The tape is removed, laid out flat, and measured. This measurement is divided by the number of positions required and each of these marked on the tape. The tape is then wrapped around the circumference of the work once more. Each of these marks now represents a center line for the rows of holes used in the shotgun muzzle brakes, or center lines for bolt lugs, or whatever. Inside divisions can be made by wrapping the tape around a shaft that fits the inside diameter closely and dividing as above. It is then inserted into the work and location marks transferred from the tape to the end of the work. This method is not intended to replace precision equipment, but if only a few such operations are to be undertaken and the equipment is not available, this method will pinpoint locations to within a very few thousandths, if care is taken.

Grinding wheels are usually too slow to shape metal parts. The sanding discs used primarily in automobile body shops are available from hardware and auto parts stores. These are fairly stiff, fiber-backed discs usually of 7- or 9-inch diameter. They are available in grits ranging from 24 to 120. A backplate just slightly smaller than the discs is made from plastic, masonite, etc. and mounted behind the disc on an arbor. Parts can be shaped to almost exact contours using this method. These are also useful when shaping wood.

Inside polishing, such as inside trigger guards and the like, is made easier by sawing a lengthwise slot in a wood dowel. Strips of abrasive cloth or paper are mounted by placing one end in the slot and winding several turns around it in the opposite direction of its rotation. A 1/2-inch drill chuck that can be mounted on a motor arbor and the dowel chucked in it is ideal for this. Use a fairly high-speed motor of 3750 RPM or similar for this.

Recoil pads mounted on the straight-line recoil type buttstocks have upper mounting screws that come out right in the place where the stock bolt hole is located. Sometimes another screw can be located higher and miss the bolt hole. It is easier to silver-solder a screw head to the end of the stock bolt that will accept an Allen wrench. The recoil pad's upper screw hole is enlarged to permit insertion of the Allen wrench and a corresponding slot cut in the face of the pad. The pad is then mounted in place using epoxy cement and the lower screw. The stock bolt is turned by inserting a long, round-bodied Allen wrench through the face of the recoil pad. If a coating of oil or grease is used to lubricate the Allen wrench, the face of the recoil pad will show little or no evidence of the wrench insertion after it is withdrawn.

Marks and scribed lines on metal are often hard to see during the sawing or milling process. A thin coal of layout fluid such as Dykem brushed on and allowed to dry for a few minutes will make subsequent lines more visible. This product is available from both machine tool and gunsmith supply houses in red, blue, or other colors. Obtain a can of remover and thinner at the same time. An even better method consists of polishing the surface of the metal bright and swabbing on a solution of copper sulfate. This will leave a thin layer of copper deposited on the surface that causes any markings to stand out vividly. Copper sulfate is a blue crystalline powder available from drug stores. It is also known at Bluestone and Blue Vitroil. The solution is made by adding all the copper sulfate that four ounces of distilled water will dissolve. Add 12 to 15 drops of sulphuric acid to this.

Years ago, a cold bluing solution that came in two bottles was marketed. The contents of the first bottle (copper sulfate) was swabbed on the clean bright steel, which imparted a thin copper layer. The contents of the second bottle, which consisted mostly of arsenic trioxide, was applied next, which turned the copper black. As I remember, it resulted in a better black color than the modern cold blues. But, like most of the others, it started to rub off in a short time. It was also one of the foulest smelling concoctions I ever came in contact with.

In many instances, silver solder will be used to mount sight bases, trigger guards, barrel bands, and various other parts. There are people who will tell you that the correct way to join parts using this material is to cut strips of the flat "ribbon" material and sandwich it between the parts to be joined, whereupon heat is applied, the solder melts, and, when cool, the joint is made. This may work for some people. Everytime I tried it, however, the results were somewhat different. When the work is clamped together and the sandwiched silver solder melted, the parts tend to shift or slip in their relationship to each other. Besides that, I was never sure that all the solder melted and flowed.

A far better method, at least for me, is to apply flux to the surfaces to be joined and clamp them together. The adjacent surfaces are rubbed down with soapstone or a soldering "talc" crayon, which will prevent the solder from adhering to the exposed surfaces. Using a wire-type silver solder of 45- to 55-percent silver content, the joint and surrounding metal is heated until it just begins to turn red and the end of the solder touched to the joint. The application of heat is continued until the molten solder is visible all around the edges, at which time the heat is withdrawn and the work allowed to cool. Care must be taken not to overheat it since silver solder has a tendency to simply evaporate when overheated, and the fumes are toxic. The joint is then cleaned of the flux and soapstone residue, and any excess material is removed using files or scrapers.

Whether we like it or not, sooner or later we will be required to turn the outside of a barrel to a specific size and contour. The easiest way, as concerns the small shop, is to mount the barrel between centers in the lathe and set the tail stock over enough to cut the appropriate taper. Since the breech end usually has a threaded shank followed by a straight tapered forward section followed by an abrupt taper or tapered curve, there is usually a length of 18 to 20 inches that consists of a straight, gradual taper usually of .150 to .200 inch over the entire length. This taper can be set up to give an almost exact measurement by mounting a dial indicator on the cross slide of the lathe and measuring the amount that the tail stock is set over. After a few passes are made with the lathe tool, and while the barrel is still oversize, the muzzle end and the point where the taper ends are measured. The amount of tail-stock set-over is changed to correct whatever error is present.

A steady rest can be used to support the barrel and dampen it to prevent chatter by offsetting the steady rest jaws to coincide with the tail stock offset, but it will require moving a couple of times. Usually there will be a slight step or ridge where the previous cut is stopped and a new one started. Therefore it is probably easier to turn the full length without using the steady rest, instead using a wood block held against the barrel to dampen the vibration and draw filing the entire length to remove tool and chatter marks, finishing with varying grits of bench strip.

When using high sights, it is extremely important that the sights stand exactly vertical, or straight up and down. This can present a problem, since these are not easy to hold in place with clamps or to determine when they are straight up. One way to do this is to clamp the receiver or barrel in the milling machine vise, making sure it is square and level. A rod with a sharp conical point is mounted in the mill collet. The sight assembly is located in place and held by pressure between the quill and mill table. A weighted string, or plumb line, is suspended from the ceiling directly in front of the work. Then, by sighting along the surface, the sight assembly can be aligned vertically with the string by moving the cross feed of the mill table until it is straight up and down, whereupon the sight assembly is silver-soldered in place.

Turning long firing pins can present a problem. The lathe tool must be sharp and set up to contact the material to be turned exactly on center. The material is mounted in the lathe with one end extending from the chuck for a short distance and the free end supported by a center. This section is turned to size, taking light shallow cuts. It is then extended further and again turned to size. This is repeated until the entire length is formed. It is then mounted in the lathe chuck with just enough extending to turn the nose to its specified diameter, and the counterstink end for the lathe center is removed. The hemispherical tip can be formed with a file and polished with abrasive cloth.

Coil springs must be supported for most of their length, either by an inside guide pin or a spring pocket enclosing most of the spring's length. Otherwise they may buckle and deform, rendering them inoperative. As used with triggers, sears, extractors, etc., spring pockets are drilled in the part to contain most of the length of the spring, thus supporting it around the outer surface. When coil springs are used as long, traveling hammer springs and the like, they must be supported by an internal guide rod. Many times, the compressed length should be taken into consideration when determining spring pocket depth and length of travel of moving parts. This is easily determined by multiplying the number of coils in the spring by the diameter of the wire that the spring is wound from.

There are times when it is important to determine thread depth, and no chart or table is on hand to refer to. The root diameter (the size of the screw shank remaining inside the threads) can be determined to within a couple of thousandths by dividing the pitch, or number of threads per inch, into 1.299. Since a 100-percent thread will not screw into a 100-percent hole, some clearance must be allowed. A 75-percent thread is an accepted standard. Therefore we would take the result of the division above and use 75 percent of it, which gives a satisfactory tap drill size or hole size in which threads will be machined.

When glass bedding or epoxy-based compounds are used to reinforce or fill gaps between wood and metal joints, it is absolutely necessary that any holes, depressions, cracks, seams, or anything else that this material may be forced into when drawn together be plugged or sealed to prevent such from occurring. Holes can be plugged with paraffin wax, cracks and seams taped over, and slots and depressions filled with wax. All surfaces except the ones the substance is to adhere to must be coated with some sort of release agent to prevent them from becoming bonded together permanently. If no commercial release agent is available, automotive paste wax can be used. Give the exposed surfaces a thin coat and let it dry, then give them another coat. All screw threads must also be coated. Antifreeze that contains glycerine can also be used for this.

Shotgun bores and chambers, as well as rifle and pistol chambers, can be polished by slotting the end of a wood dowel, inserting one end of a strip of abrasive cloth or paper in the slot, and winding it around the dowel in the direction the work rotates. With the barrel held in the lathe chuck, the cutting end of the dowel is inserted in the bore, the lathe turned on, and the hand-held dowel moved slowly back and forth through the bore. The abrasive material should be a snug fit in the bore and will require frequent replacement. A final polish should be applied using 400 grit (wet or dry) paper followed by crocus cloth. Lubricant is used throughout the process. Chambers can be polished in the same manner by using correspondingly sized dowels. This is, more or less, a makeshift operation to be used in the absence of commercial hones and polishing heads. However if sufficient time and effort is invested, it will give good results.

When barrels are installed, either in receivers or mated to barrel extensions, they must be drawn up tight. When mated to a receiver, this is easily accomplished using a barrel vise and an action wrench. The barrel extension sometimes presents problems since it is difficult to fasten onto with a means to turn it. One way to tighten or remove it is to bore a pair of hardwood blocks to the same diameter as the extension. A clamp is made with a bolt on each side to fit over and contain the blocks. One leg of this clamp is either long enough to serve as a handle or turned to fit inside a length of pipe, which serves as a handle. This is used in the same manner as an action wrench.

Flat parts can be polished while retaining flat sides and sharp edges by placing abrasive cloth or paper on a sheet of plate glass and rubbing the part to be polished back and forth across it. As usual, progressively finer abrasive grits are used, as well as cutting oil.

Holes can be drilled or bored in the lathe and

shoulders and threads can be cut to exact depth by mounting a dial indicator on the lathe bed in a location where the stylus will contact the lathe carriage as it reaches the bottom of the cut. The indicator should be set up to stop on a number after the indicating hand has traversed the dial a couple of times, not just as contact is made. This will give ample warning before the stopping point is reached.

There are times when slots must be cut that cannot be reached with ordinary milling cutters. It is also difficult to cut such slots with a hacksaw, since succeeding saw cuts tend to slip over into the adjacent cut. If the mounting pins in the hacksaw are replaced with longer pins, more than one blade can be mounted simultaneously in the saw frame. This will allow wider slots to be cut at one time, with the slot width regulated by the number of blades used.

Most feeding problems in box-magazine guns can be alleviated by reshaping the magazine lips and/or follower. If the nose of the cartridge or shell tries to contact the top of the chamber before entering, the magazine lips should be bent inward slightly. Reshaping the follower so that the forward end rides lower in the magazine may also correct this. If the shell hits at the bottom, the magazine lips are spread slightly or the follower is bent to ride lower at the rear. Sometimes the cartridge nose will hang on the left or right sides. This can usually be corrected by bending the lip slightly upward on the side the bullet should be steered toward, or by bending the opposite side downward.

When small boring bars are needed for use in the lathe and none are available, end mills can be mounted in the tool post (especially a four-way tool post) and one flute used as a cutting edge. The body should be angled just enough to provide clearance. You can't bore deep cavities with these, but they work in a pinch.

To obtain a good finish when turning plastic, as with forends, a sharp, round-nosed tool should be used. It should have twice as much clearance as used for cutting steel and no rake. The material is turned at a fairly high speed and fed slowly. This material must not be allowed to overheat since the surface tends to melt, spoiling the finished surface. Therefore, friction, the primary cause of heating, must be kept to a minimum.

Chapter

Actions

7

Rifles and shotguns can have autoloading or automatic actions, slide actions, lever actions, bolt actions, single-shot actions, and multiple-barrel actions, or be muzzle loaders. These same action types, with the addition of revolvers, have been used in pistol actions. Of late, a few shotguns and rifles have again surfaced with revolving cylinders, but most didn't last long. There were also revolving rifles and shotguns built back in the 1800s, but they went the same way as their modern counterparts. Gas leakage between the barrel and cylinder gap was one reason for their demise. Weak frames was another.

There are several different types of autoloading actions. In the locked-breech category, there are short recoil, long recoil, gas operated, inertia locked, and hesitation locked. The unlocked, or blowback as they are usually called, actions have no mechanical lock. The weight of the bolt, or breechblock, in combination with spring pressure holds the bolt closed at the instant of firing, hopefully

until the bullet is well up the bore and pressure has diminished.

These fall into two categories: closed bolt and open bolt. Closed-bolt guns are striker fired or fired by a separate hammer. The bolt remains closed until fired, at which time it travels to the rear, extracting and ejecting the empty case, until it is arrested by the return, or recoil, spring. It is then pushed forward by the compressed spring, picking up and chambering a fresh cartridge. The bolt then remains closed until fired again.

The open-bolt gun usually has a fixed firing pin machined into the bolt face. The bolt is held in its open position until the moment of firing, at which time pulling the trigger allows it to slam forward, picking up and chambering a cartridge as it moves forward, until the cartridge seats in the chamber and the firing pin slams into the primer, firing the round. The bolt then travels to the rear, extracting and ejecting the empty case, where the sear engages and holds the bolt open until the gun is again fired. This type of gun is usually inaccurate, partially due to the hard,

Centerfire blowback action.

Inertia-locked autoloading blowback action.

Blowback pistol trigger assembly.

lengthy trigger pull found on most of these guns but mainly due to the disturbing motion of the heavy bolt slamming forward between the time the trigger is pulled and the instant of firing.

These blowback type actions are only suitable for low-powered cartridges and should not be considered for any other use.

Likewise, most short-recoil actions are only suitable for low-powered cartridges and should not be considered for any other use. Short-recoil actions are so named because the breech is locked at the instant of firing, and the bolt and barrel then travel together for a short distance to the rear until the bolt is unlocked, usually by some sort of cam or toggle action. This allows it to continue its travel to the rear while the barrel is stopped and moves forward again when the bolt returns forward, thereby locking the breech once more. The Browning-type autoloading pistols as made by Colt, Smith and Wesson, Ruger, and others are examples of this type of action.

Long-recoil actions work in much the same way, except that the barrel and bolt travel as a locked assembly most of the way to the rear, where unlocking takes place. The barrel then moves forward while the bolt is held to the rear for a short interval, then allowed to move forward. Browning A5 shotguns, among others, are an example of this.

The gas-operated action is considered superi-

or to either of these, mostly because the barrel is fixed in the frame and does not move. This type action normally has one or more gas ports positioned somewhere near midway between the chamber and muzzle of the barrel. Gas passing through the port(s) pushes against a piston, which is connected in some way to the bolt. This opens the bolt far enough to unlock it, after which recoil and residual gas pressure cause it to continue its rearward travel until stopped by the compressed recoil spring, which then pushes it forward to the locked position once more. These gas-operated actions usually will do more toward recoil reduction than the other types. Many modern autoloading centerfire rifles and shotguns use this system.

The inertia-locked action also features a non-moving fixed barrel. As used, the heavy bolt surrounds a bolthead with a heavy spring between them. When the gun is fired, either the bolt stands still and the rest of the gun recoils to the rear, compressing the spring, or the bolt jumps, forward compressing the spring. I have never been entirely sure just which action takes place, but anyway, the spring ends up compressed. Then the compressed spring kicks the bolt to the rear, causing it to unlock, and inertia, recoil, and residual gas pressure cause it to continue to the rear until the compressed recoil spring stops it and pushes it back forward to the

Shotgun bolt with rotating bolthead.

Rising-block shotgun bolt.

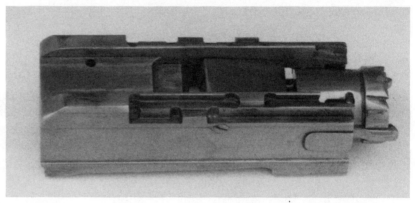

locked position. While this is a simple action that requires less parts to make it work, it depends on recoil to make it function. I built several autoloading shotguns and some self-opening trap guns using this type action, and they worked perfectly. But when I attempted to cut down on the excessive amount of recoil generated by adding muzzle brakes, spring-loaded stocks, overboring, etc., the action would no longer open completely.

Benelli shotguns use an action of this type. But they use a tight bore some .005 to .006 inch smaller than the standard .729-inch 12 gauge bore to generate enough recoil to make them work dependably. This results is an accelerated recoil level, making the Benelli guns some of the hardest kicking guns on the market.

Then there is a locking system usually referred to as a hesitation lock. Here again, there is a heavy bolt surrounding a separate bolthead.

Between the two are a pair of rollers that are pushed outward into engagement with corresponding depressions in either the receiver walls or a barrel extension when the bolt body is all the way forward, more or less locking the action. Upon firing, the rollers remain cammed in the locked position until recoil moves the bolt slightly to the rear. At this point the rollers collapse inward, allowing the bolt to proceed to the rear unimpeded except for the compression of the recoil spring.

The drawback to this system is that in some cases it doesn't remain locked long enough. Most of the firearms using this locking system attempt to control premature opening of the bolt by cutting shallow grooves, or flutes, lengthwise in the chamber walls. Some will tell you that the added friction caused by pressure forcing the case walls into these grooves hold the case in place longer. Others say that the grooves allow gas to flow

.22 blowback action.

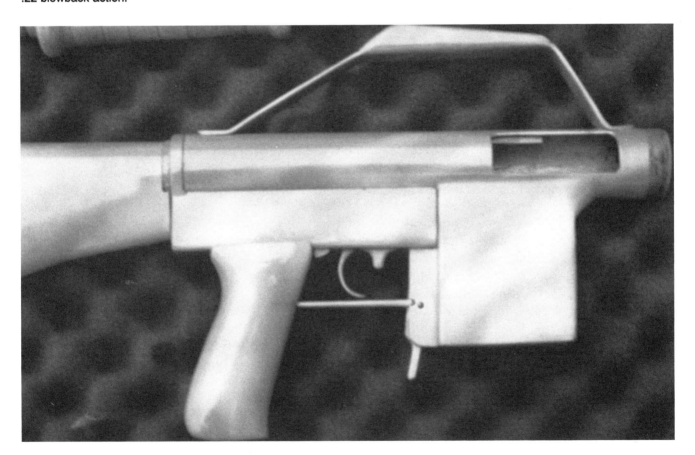

Slide-action 12-gauge.

Self-opening trap gun action.

between the case and chamber walls, "floating" the case and permitting easy extraction even though chamber pressure is still high. Most Heckler & Koch firearms use this locking system.

Slide, or pump, actions work in much the same way as the autoloaders except that the bolt is moved back and forth manually through use of a reciprocating slide handle, or forend. These usually lock either by means of a rotating bolt-head or a rising block. Either of these mates with corresponding recesses in a barrel extension. There have also been designs in which the rear end of the bolt tips up or down into a recess in the receiver to lock.

In many cases, the same bolt and receiver used in the autoloader can also be used in the slide action. This is especially true with the gas-operated autoloader, in that the gas ports, piston, recoil spring, etc. are eliminated from the design. The slide handle connected to the operating bar(s) is in its place.

The bolt action has long been considered the strongest and most accurate of the lot. But if

locking lugs of equal size and quality of material are used, there is no reason why the slide action or autoloader with a rotating bolthead should not be equally strong and capable of containing an equal amount of pressure. The main reason for the bolt action's superior accuracy lies in its one-piece stock. This allows bedding the action solidly in the stock while permitting varying amounts of pressure or support to be exerted against the barrel by the forend, or, in some cases, letting the barrel float free with no interference from the forend whatsoever.

Most bolt actions are of the turn-bolt variety. These will have one or more locking lugs spaced around the circumference of the bolt body. While usually found at the front, several designs have these lugs at the rear end of the bolt. Some even use the root of the bolt handle as the locking lug. For years, the standard for military and sporting actions was two locking lugs spaced 180 degrees apart and located just behind the bolt face. Several also had an auxiliary, or safety, lug located close to the rear of the bolt in case the other two failed.

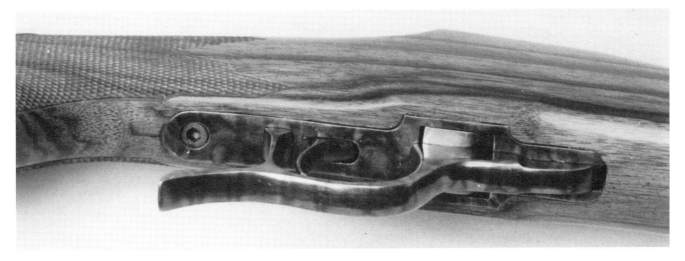

Bottom side of falling block.

Falling block action with square breechblock.

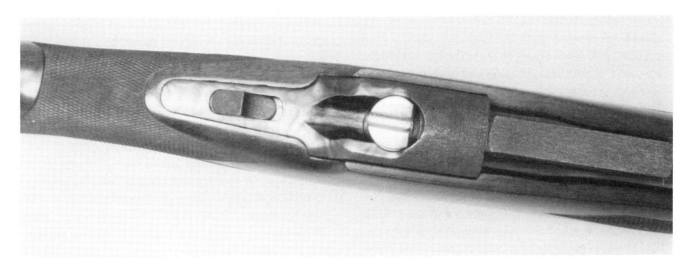

Falling-block action with round breechblock.

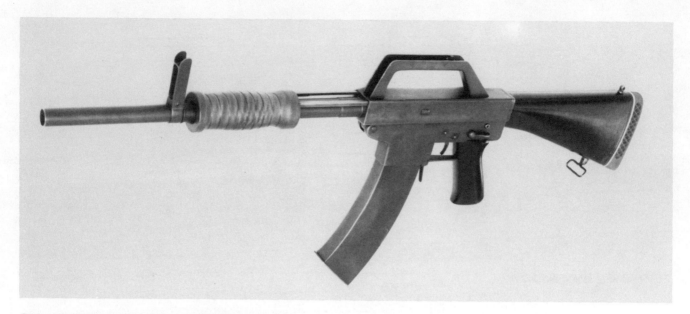

Slide-action 12-gauge shotgun with square receiver.

The lugs extended outward and were considerably larger in diameter than the bolt body, requiring raceways cut most of the length of the receiver to allow the lugs to move back and forth.

In recent years, a number of designs have appeared with three or more lugs spaced equidistantly around the bolt body with the lugs of the same diameter. This eliminates the need for bolt raceways cut in the receiver. The more lugs that are used, the less bolt lift is required (two lugs require a 90-degree bolt lift, three require 60, and four require 45), but the shorter bolt lift requires a steeper angle in the cocking cam. This can result in considerably more effort required to lift the bolt in a three- or four-lug action than needed with the two-lug job.

There are also straight pull designs, which may have a rotating bolthead operated by cam action or a cross bolt that locks through both sides of the receiver. I made several trap guns based on the straight pull cross-bolt action. Browning also built a gun they called a "T bolt" that had a similar action. They offered no advantage over the turn bolt.

Lever actions are only used on rifles at present. Winchester made shotguns years ago, and Marlin also made a few, as well as at least one other firm. They couldn't compete with the slide action, however, and gradually faded away. The more modern lever actions have either rotating boltheads that lock at the front just behind the barrel or locking bolts located at the rear of the action which ride in slots in the frame and engage into slots in the bolt, locking both together. Several reproduction rifles are available, duplicating Henry and early Winchesters, that use the original-style toggle link lock. These are not suitable for high-pressure cartridges.

Single-shot actions, that concern us here, can be classified as falling-block actions and break-open actions. The break-open actions usually hinge in the middle just ahead of the trigger guard. Several different types of locking bolts are used to lock the barrel assembly in place against the frame. This bolt is normally withdrawn by pressing a top lever crosswise. This type of action, properly made, is suitable for use with any cartridge made for a shoulder-fired firearm.

The falling-block action uses a lever-actuated breechblock that slides up and down in the receiver, closing and opening the breech end of the barrel. Both these and the break-open action usually incorporate an automatic ejector that throws the empty case out of the chamber when the gun is opened after firing. Both types are usually hammer fired and contain very few moving parts. The falling-block action, properly designed and built, is suitable for use with high-pressure cartridges.

Multiple barrel firearms are almost always built on break-open actions. Barrel arrangement will be either side by side or over and under.

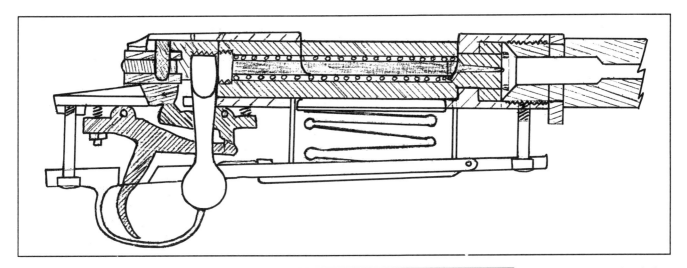

Turn-bolt, magazine-fed action.

Single-shot, falling-block action.

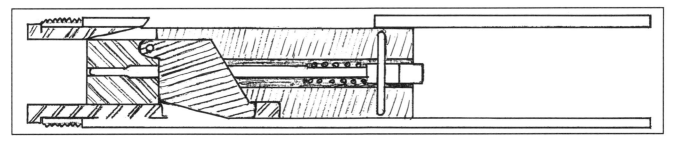

Rising-block action shown in 12-gauge dimensions. It can be used in automatic, slide action, or straight pull.

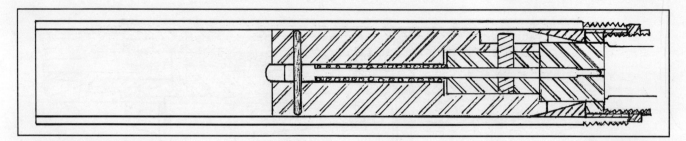

Rotating bolthead action as used in 12-gauge shotgun. It can be automatic, slide action, or straight pull and is adaptable to other calibers and gauges.

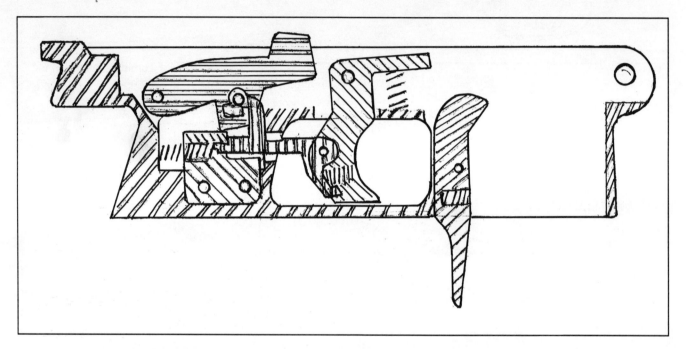

Open-bolt, blowback, .22 pistol trigger assembly.

These actions hinge and lock in the same way the single-shot break actions do. Used primarily in shotguns, these actions are also used in double rifles that can be in any caliber used in shoulder-fired firearms.

There is too much handwork and fitting involved in making a gun like this for it to be profitable in a small shop. I designed and built a double rifle once. It was almost 20 years ago. It took me over six months to build it. I never got a dime for it. After shooting it a few times, I let a friend (?) of mine take it to the west coast to display it at a gun show. He was going to promote it and form a company to produce it in quantity. I never saw him, or the gun, again.

Multiple-barrel guns also exist in three- or four-barrel configurations. This includes four shotgun barrels with two directly above the other two, or one barrel directly under and between the upper side-by-side barrels. These can and have been made with shotgun barrels in combination with rifle barrels too, such as rifle barrels along side and between over-and-under shotgun barrels. These are only a some of the combinations that have been dreamed up. Like the double rifles, these are too time consuming to make a profit on. But I have made all sorts of guns before that I didn't get anything for, so I may try one of these sometime, just to show people that I can.

Of the action types described in this chapter, the autoloader, slide action, and bolt action are the easiest to manufacture in the small shop.

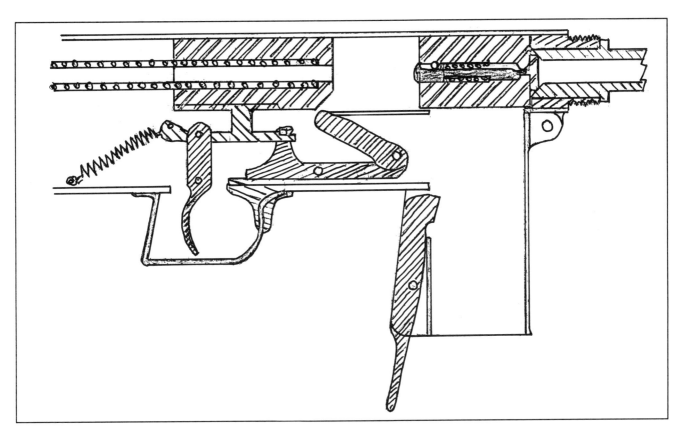

Closed-bolt blowback action for low-pressure cartridges only.

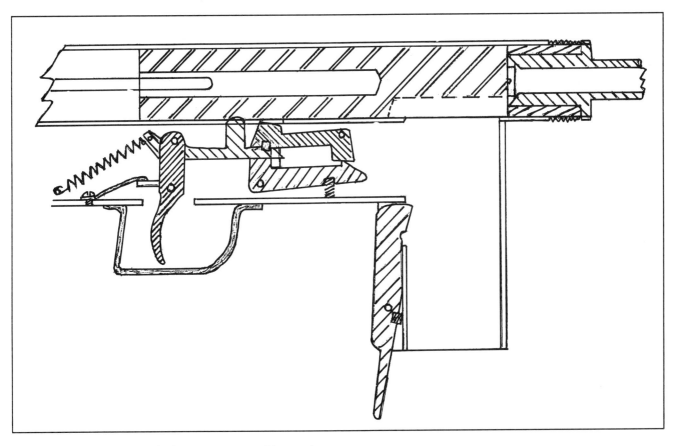

Open-bolt blowback action for low-pressure cartridges only.

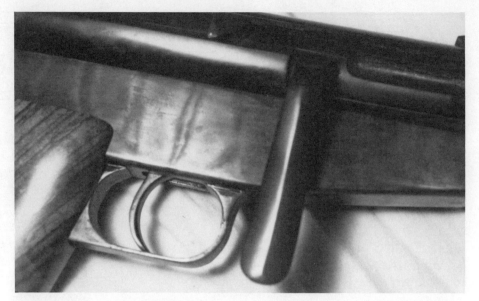

Single-shot bolt action.

Upper receiver separated from lower.

Bolt (right).

End view of the bolt.
The locking lugs
and ejector are
visible (far right).

Receivers can be fabricated from round seamless aircraft grade tubing known as 4130. It is also referred to as chrome moly by aircraft mechanics and fabricators. This material can be obtained in almost any size and wall thickness desired at least close enough to adapt to your usage.

When using such tubing for receivers, round solid stock such as 4140-4150 or similar compositions can be obtained in sizes that will require only a light lathe cut, at most, to slide back and forth inside the tubing. The firing pin hole, bolt face cuts, and any relief cuts are far more easily located and centered using round stock than when square or rectangular bolts are used. This should be kept in mind when designing the firearm, since quite a bit of fabrication time can be saved.

Lower receivers, trigger housings, magazine housings, etc., can be bent to shape from sheet metal. Triggers, hammers, and the like can be sawn to shape as closely as possible from flat stock and finished by milling, filing, and grinding.

Lever actions, single shots, and multibarrel receivers require machining from rectangular material. While some of the excess material can be removed from the exterior by sawing, extensive mill work is required to form the inside surfaces. This can be expensive, both material and time wise. It is recommended that the round receiver and bolt-type designs be used if possible.

We will look at actual designs using these principles later in the book.

Action Fabrication

8

Much time and machine work can be saved by selecting an action design that incorporates a receiver made from tubing. Several of these have been described in other parts of this book. Actions of this type can be adapted to rifle, shotgun, or pistol applications by changing the dimensions slightly.

The tubing diameter and wall thickness can be as small as 7/8 inch outside diameter with .059 inch wall thickness for .22 rimfire applications; 1 1/4 inch outside diameter with .065 inch wall thickness for centerfire pistol cartridges; and 1 1/2 inch outside diameter with .120 inch wall thickness for 12-gauge shotguns and centerfire rifle cartridges.

Magazine housings, if for a multishot firearm, can be formed separately and pinned or bolted to the receiver. They can also be folded from sheet metal and welded in place. While either method is acceptable, a stiffer assembly will result if the welded-on housing is used.

With the thinner tubing, barrel bushings should be turned to a push fit inside the receiver and welded in place. Neater welds will result if 1/4-inch holes are drilled equidistantly around the circumference of the receiver, just behind the front edge, and the bushing welded in place through these holes. Each weld is then dressed flush with the surface, leaving no evidence of such a weld ever having been made. The barrel bushing will require threading to accept a barrel retaining nut, or sleeve. Thicker-walled receivers are threaded directly for the nut.

Overall length is dictated by the length of the bolt and the cartridge used. It must be long enough to allow the front face of the bolt to move to the rear far enough to pick up cartridges from the magazine. This can range from as little as an 1 1/2 inch for pistol cartridges to 3 1/2 inches for certain rifle and shotgun cartridges.

An opening for the magazine must be cut in the appropriate location on the lower side and an ejection port just above it. Also, slots are needed to clear the hammer, ejector, and disconnector, if one is used. In certain applications, the back end of the receiver is threaded and an end cap threaded to match. Most designs will also require a block welded to the bottom side at the rear, which is drilled and tapped for a grip and lower receiver mounting bolt. Some of these require a similar block at the front for a crosspin or screw. A sight base is mounted on the top rear when used as a pistol. Rifles and riot-type shotguns will have a combination sight base and carrying handle mounted. A single-shot trap gun will use an adjustable sighting rib. These are either welded or silver-soldered in place.

Bolts are made using appropriate round stock turned to a size that will slide freely through the receiver tube. If used in an autoloading blowback type, no locking lugs will be necessary since the bolt weight and pressure from the recoil spring(s) are depended on to keep the bolt closed until pressure has diminished.

Any manually operated action, even a .22 rimfire, will require some means to lock it shut. Probably the easiest way to accomplish this, at least the most uncomplicated way, is through use of a rotating bolt, or in some cases, bolthead. This is accomplished by machining a predetermined number of locking lugs around the circumference of the bolt, which mate with matching surfaces in the receiver or barrel extension. The number of locking lugs used is a matter of choice. With low-powered cartridges only one small lug may be required. For over a century, two fairly large lugs have been used in conventional bolt-action rifles. However, as has been mentioned elsewhere, less bolt lift will be required if more lugs are used.

If a turn-bolt action is used in the designs presented here, the locking lugs will be machined to match cuts in a barrel extension. The cocking cam must be aligned with the slot in the receiver wall that the bolt handle reciprocates in. The extended guide portion of the cocking piece also rides in this slot. Due to the large diameter of the bolt body, the cocking cam slot can still be quite shallow, even with multiple lugs, which lessens the effort needed to open the bolt with the firing pin in its forward position. It is recommended that four lugs be used, as it will require only half as much bolt rotation to unlock the action as would a two-lug bolt.

A bolt handle can be joined to the bolt body by drilling a crosswise hole through the bolt body at the point where the bolt handle is to be located. A stub is turned on a bolt handle blank, leaving it .006 to .008 inch larger than the diameter of the hole through the bolt. This blank is placed in a freezer overnight, which will cause it to shrink slightly. Just before installation, the bolt body is heated, which, in turn, will expand it slightly. It isn't necessary to heat it to a point where it changes color; it will expand at a fairly low temperature. Then, before it has a chance to cool, the stub of the handle is started in the hole and, using a heavy hammer, driven entirely through the bolt body. When the assembly thus made cools and warms to room temperature, the heated part will shrink and the cold part will expand slightly, resulting in a joint almost as solid as if welded. The bolt handle is then machined and bent to the desired shape. A close-fitting crosspin can be installed to hold it in place if desired, but it is not necessary.

As used in an autoloading or slide-action design, a separate bolthead is used that incorporates the locking lugs. The lugs are rotated by an angled cam cut in the bolt body, which bears against a pin projecting from the bolt head, and cams it into rotation through forward and rearward movement of the bolt body. This in turn is connected to a forend (if a slide action) or a gas piston sleeve (if an autoloader) by a wide action bar.

When used in low-powered single-locking-lug guns, the entire bolt can be made in one piece, wherein the entire unit will rotate to accomplish locking and unlocking.

It is also possible to use square tubing in the fabrication of receivers. My own shotguns were originally built in such a manner. This was done because I couldn't figure out a way to connect the bolt to the action bar in a round-receiver gun. These are harder to machine than the ones with round receivers. A plug must be made from square stock to be welded inside the front end of the receiver. This requires a hole bored through the exact center and threaded, plus the feeding or approach cone and locking recesses machined in one end.

The bolt was also made from square stock. A hole was bored through it for the firing pin and rotating bolthead. In several blowback versions it was required that a small firing pin hole be drilled in one end, then the material reversed and a larger hole for the firing pin body and spring drilled from the other end. These holes, to be satisfactory, had to be concentric and meet exactly. In a small shop, one is required to use a lathe equipped with a four-jaw chuck for this, mounting the work and centering it through use of a dial indicator. This isn't actually too difficult, but it takes time.

There are armchair machinists who will tell you that if you only loosen two adjacent jaws of the four-jaw chuck to reverse or replace the material, it will go back exactly centered simply by tightening these same two jaws. I must have read a different book, because I could never do this. Even when I used a torque wrench and tightened them exactly the same each time, the work was always off some and required centering again. Not long ago, by chance, one of these experts came into my shop and started telling me how easy it was to center square stock and repeat it as above. I tried to get him to show me, but when it didn't work for him either, he went off mumbling that there was something wrong with my lathe chuck.

One day it occurred to me that by using a takedown barrel that was held in place by a screw-on collar and removing the entire assembly—barrel, action bar, bolt, and all—from the front of the receiver, I could use a round receiver after all. This didn't actually reduce the amount of machine work by much, but it virtually eliminated the time required in centering it, as was required with the square stock. Since that time, my own receivers have been made from round stock.

The lower receiver can be folded from sheet metal or machined from solid stock. If formed from sheet metal, both ends will require a filler block welded in place. The one at the back end can be thin since it simply closes the opening, but the one at the front must be long enough to contain a recess for the receiver mounting block to fit into.

When formed to a size and shape that suits you, the upper edges must be machined flat and square and the inside cut to the same radius as the receiver. This is best done by using a ball cutter of the same diameter as the upper receiver. A cap to fit against the rear of the receiver is turned to size, with a hole drilled and tapped for the stock bolt, and welded in place at the rear of the lower receiver. This can be located exactly by placing the cap between the upper and lower receivers. With both of these and the end cap located where you want them, clamp them together, holding the cap in place. It is now welded along both sides and across the back.

If a bolt slot is cut from the ejection port entirely through the rear end as will be required to allow installation and removal of the bolt in the bolt-action gun, the end cap should be left solid across the top to keep the bolt slot from spreading. When used with the others, where the rear end of the tubing remains solid, the upper half of the thin portion of the cap can be cut away. This will permit the rear end of the receiver to lift straight up, pivoting around the front mounting screw.

At least one of the trigger mechanisms described in the trigger chapter can be adapted for use in the actions described here. In certain cases, a trigger guard is cut to shape and welded or silver soldered to the lower side of the receiver.

Double extractors should be installed in shotguns and guns firing other rimmed case calibers. Actually the term "double" or "dual" extractors is slightly misleading. The outside extractor does all the work; the inside one holds the shell head in place against the bolt face and prevents it from slipping out from under the extractor proper.

An ejector must be located where it will contact the casehead, throwing the empty case out of the gun just as soon as the action is open far enough for the case to miss the breech end of the barrel. Ideally it will be located just below the inboard extractor and project through the bolt face just inside the outer diameter.

Those little spring-loaded ejectors that are pinned into the face of the bolt should be avoided if possible. These project from the bolt face until forced back, compressing the spring when the bolt is closed with a shell in the chamber. Therefore the casehead cannot slide up under the extractors as it is being fed from the magazine. Instead it must be pushed into the chamber ahead of the extractors because the protruding ejector won't let it move up across the bolt face. Thus these extractors are required to jump over the case rim. They are also apt to malfunction when dirty.

I have seen these ejectors get foreign material under them, or rust, which prevents the bolt from closing on the cartridge. Once a friend of mine went all the way to Alaska and couldn't use his gun because of this very thing. He brought it to me, telling me the "headspace grew." When I showed him what the trouble was, he traded the gun for a rifle with a Mauser action and swore that he would never own another like it.

Several of the trigger assemblies described will allow placement of a sliding safety just forward of the trigger. As far as I am concerned (and many others confirm this), this is the ideal location for the safety since it is equally accessible to the trigger finger of either hand.

When the rotating bolthead is used, a guide rail must be riveted or welded inside the receiver at the top to hold the bolthead in the open position as the bolt moves back and forth. Without this, resistance to the bolt feeding a shell from the magazine will try to force the bolthead into the locked position. The bolthead must be held in the open position until the lugs actually start into the lug raceways.

The single-shot falling-block action has appeal to a number of people, especially to admirers of the "classic" style custom rifles. The biggest drawback to building these in a small shop is the amount of machine work involved. If produced in sufficient quantities, investment castings could be produced which would reduce machining time considerably. If cast slightly oversize and finish ground, the appearance would not suffer.

The first step, after acquiring a suitable length of rectangular material, is to mount it in the four-jaw chuck and, when centered, bore a hold for the barrel tenon. This should be bored with an undersize drill, which will also form the cartridge feed trough directly behind the breechblock opening. The hole is then enlarged to the root diameter of the thread to a depth slightly deeper than the length of the barrel tenon and threaded using a small inside threading tool. The threading should be finished and the face cut square before the material is removed from the lathe.

The receiver blank is removed from the chuck and remounted with the surface that will ultimately be the bottom side facing outward. An opening for the breechblock is located and centered. It is then drilled completely through and bored to size. If a round breechblock (which is

suitable for low- to medium-pressure cartridges only) is to be used, a counterbore to accept a tubular breechblock guide is bored 1/8 inch deep.

If a square breechblock, which will withstand high pressures, is used, the opening is bored as above. It can be machined square, except for the rounded corners, with an end mill. The corners can be cut square by filing or broaching. By making a filler block to just fit the opening and leaving a flange at the upper side to keep it in place, and slots cut along the corners for a broach to slide through, the inside corners can be cut square by pushing or pulling the broach through the opening.

All excess material is then removed by sawing and/or milling, and the receiver formed to shape. A slot is cut through the upper tang for the safety lever and a wider recess for the safety slide.

The lower receiver is cut from a separate piece of flat stock and the breechblock opening made. If the round breechblock is used, the opening is counterbored on the upper side for the tubular breechblock guide. With the guide in place and used as a spacer and locating point, holes for the action screws can be drilled and tapped. For appearance sake, the rear action screw hole should not be drilled cmpletely through the upper tang.

The breechblock is machined to a slip fit inside the receiver opening. Slots are cut for the lever and hammer clearance and the front side machined to mate against the breech end of the barrel. The barrel can be fitted and chambered at this time.

Small parts, including the lever, hammer, trigger, safety, and ejector, are laid out and cut from flat stock. They are then finished and fitted in place. A lengthwise slot must be cut in the bottom left side of the receiver to accept the ejector, which is pinned in place. A relief cut must also be made in the end of the barrel to accept the ejector blade.

This action will require quite a bit of hand fitting to work properly. When fitted and assembled, the breechblock should open easily until the chamber is exposed. A harder pull downward on the lever releases the ejector, which throws the empty cartridge case out of the gun. The lever is then pulled upward slightly, which cams the ejector back into the breech face and latches it. Lowering the lever until it meets resistance from the cocked hammer should align the groove in the top of the breechblock with the chamber opening, whereby dropping a cartridge in the feed groove and tilting the muzzle downward causes the cartridge to slide forward into the chamber. The lever is then pulled upward until it latches and the gun is ready to fire.

The barrelled action must be completely inletted into the stock before the firing pin hole is drilled. This is because the breechblock may not fit in exactly the same relationship as it does when out of the stock. The hole location is marked as described ealier in the book.

A single-shot bolt-action trap gun is made by threading a 9 1/2 inch length of 1 1/2 inch outside diameter tubing, having a wall thickness of .120 inch, at the forward end to accept a barrel retaining nut. The bolt is made from 4140 or similar round stock. Four locking lugs are machined at the forward end, which mate with recesses in a barrel extension. The bolt handle is attached as described earlier. A block is welded or silver soldered to the bottom of the receiver to house either the number five trigger or, in case a release trigger is desired, the number nine trigger described in Chapter 12. A block is welded in place at the lower front to receive the lower receiver mounting cross bolt.

A lower receiver is machined from a solid block—the end cap welded in place at the top rear and a trigger guard on the bottom.

Two extractors are located 180 degrees apart at the bolt face, and an ejector is located so that it just pushes the front end of the case out of the ejection port when the bolt is retracted.

The adjustable rear sight platform is silver soldered in place atop the receiver. There are those who would have you believe that no rear sight or, as used here, reference point is desirable or necessary. This may be true for certain experts. But this requires the shooter's eye to serve as the rear sight. Unless his (or her) face is positioned exactly the same in relation to the stock for each shot, the gun will throw the pattern in a slightly different place. Therefore I suggest that the rear sight be used on the gun. It can always be removed or depressed into its lowest position for the shooter who doesn't want it.

Chapter

Barrels

9

As long as they remain available, rifle and pistol barrels should be purchased as either preturned or cylindrical blanks from one of the several manufacturers offering these products. A considerable amount of specialized equipment and tooling is required to bore, ream, and rifle a bore. This can cost an enormous amount of money that can be better spent elsewhere. It also requires extensive experience to produce consistently accurate barrels. And since the prototype rifle or pistol will have to be as accurate, or more so, than its contemporaries if we intend to market it, we should go with the best available. If one of the preturned contours can be adapted to the design used, quite a bit of machining time can be saved. If not, either a contoured blank of sufficient diameter to turn to the required contour and size or a cylindrical blank must be used. It should be noted that several of the larger manufacturers also buy their barrels from these companies.

Shotgun barrels are a different story. Very few

barrel makers offer shotgun blanks. Several years ago I obtained a number of these from a maker who swore that they were equal to or better than commercial quality. They did have a fairly good interior finish, which I enhanced by lapping. The outsides were also reasonably well done, although not even close to the dimensions specified. When I cut some of them off to reduce the length, I discovered that they were not concentric; one side would be thicker than the other. This was not necessarily unusual. Many commercial shotguns have this same problem, which is usually only discovered if the barrel is cut off to shorten it. But these barrels were also very soft. I was told they were made of "1037 carbon steel." I installed screw-in chokes and after a few hundred shots, bulges developed just behind the choke tubes. I complained about this to the barrel maker, but they said I had installed the choke tubes improperly and it was my own problem.

I started making my own barrels from 4130 seamless tubing and my "problem" disappeared. I never had another bulged barrel. I

Choke tubes add versatility. They can range from cylinder bore to full choke (right).

Slots in end are for tightening too (below left).

These tubes are full, modified, and improved cylinder (below middle).

A quarter can be used to tighten or loosen choke tubes (below right).

have never bought anything else from that barrel supplier either.

It was learned several years ago, through my own experiments and those of others, that a larger-than-standard shotgun bore not only has less recoil, but more velocity and tighter patterns than the barrels with the standard .729-.730 inch bore diameter in a 12-gauge gun. This is essentially the result of reduced friction and less shot deformation. Barrels that have larger diameters than standard barrels are commonly referred to as "overbored" or "backbored," depending on who does the referring.

A standard-size tubing (4130) is available from steel companies nationwide in 1 1/8-inch outside diameter, has a .188-inch wall thickness, and a bore diameter of .749 inch. This is ideal for the 12-gauge barrels described here. This same tubing is available in a 1.0-inch diameter, a wall

thickness of .188 inch, and a bore diameter of .624 inch, which will work in a 20-gauge barrel.

As used on the military and police or "assault" guns, a cylinder bore (no choke constriction) is desirable. So we have no problem with choke. If used in trap, skeet, or sporting shotgun barrels, however, varying degrees of choke are not only desirable but, in the case of the trap gun, mandatory. While it is possible to roll or swage choke into the end of the barrel, the simplest and most desirable solution is to install screw-in chokes. While most shotgun makers charge extra for guns so equipped, in our case it is the easiest way.

Since we are using an oversize bore, we will be required to make our own choke tubes. The standard-size choke tubes used by most manufacturers measure 13/16 inch (.8125 inch) in outside diameter in 12-gauge and are threaded 32 threads per inch. The 20-gauge tubes are 11/16 inch (.6875 inch) in diameter, with 32 threads per inch.

I used these tubes for years in my own overbored barrels without mishap. Then one day I picked up a catalog from a well-known gunsmith supply house and found that these self-proclaimed experts had ordained that you cannot install screw-in chokes in a 12-gauge barrel with a bore diameter over .735 inch or .624 inch in the 20 gauge. It goes on to say that exceeding these dimensions WILL CAUSE DAMAGED CHOKE TUBES and LIKELY CAUSE A BARREL BLOWOUT. It was probably because I hadn't read this before, but I had never had a problem with this. But then, I used a gun with damascus barrels for years before I read that they would blow up in your hands if fired. So apparently ignorance is bliss.

I find the above hard to believe, especially if the tubes are installed concentric to and in line with the bore. The standard choke tube of .8125-inch diameter is .0625 inch larger than our .750-inch bore. It has a wall thickness of .03125 inch. These same people sell what they call "thin wall" choke tubes measuring .775 inch in diameter and threaded 44 threads per inch to be installed in barrels with bore diameters of .729-.730 inch. Since these tubes only have a thickness of .023 inch, why aren't they also dangerous? And who appointed these people to make the rules?

I have gone along with this, though, simply because anyone who has read their minimum requirements and damages a choke tube or barrel for whatever reason is going to swear that it was my doing because I violated the "rules." The tubes I use now are 53/64 inch (.8285 inch) in diameter and threaded 32 threads per inch. These are not available commercially, so I am required to make them myself. It is extra trouble, but I've decided not to take any chances. Now that an "expert" has informed me that the old way was unsafe, they would probably start blowing up on me. I still shoot a damascus barrel on occasion, though.

Before we leave the subject of overbored barrels and choke tubes, it should be mentioned that 12-gauge barrels have been made with bores of .800 inch or more. A conversion that has been popular for some time now features a bore diameter of .780 inch. In effect, what this amounts to is a 10-gauge barrel shooting 12-gauge shells. These, apparently, don't have much recoil and pattern well, but several people who have owned them tell me that they have had trouble with wads not sealing, especially in cold weather. Another shooter who has one of these guns recently told me that his gun shot low, and when he tried to bend the barrel (as shooters are prone to do) to make it shoot higher, it collapsed because the barrel walls were so thin. So it may very well be that some of these overbored barrels have been overbored a little too much.

If the muzzle brake described herein is used in conjunction with one of the .750-inch bored barrels, tighter patterns than normal will be realized. The first time I patterned one of these muzzle-braked guns, I had a choke tube with .030-inch constriction in the gun. In a standard gun barrel, I would have expected this combination to put 70 to 75 percent of the shot in a 30-inch circle at 40 yards. To my surprise, it put 100 percent of the shot in a 24-inch circle. I made up some more choke tubes and discovered that .015-inch constriction gave about the 70 percent that I expected in the first place.

Further experimentation with this and subsequent guns led us to the conclusion that the gas bleed-off before the shot charge entered the choke caused the tighter patterns. This conclusion was reinforced by several paragraphs in Tom Swearengen's book, *The World's Fighting Shotguns*. On page 456, Swearengen states that a Winchester engineer decided that poor buckshot patterns were caused by dense propelling gas turbulence acting to unbalance shot wads as they emerged from the gun muzzle. This guy cut six equally spaced slots 4 inches long and .025 inch wide behind the muzzle. His patterns also tightened significantly, just as mine did.

To make a shotgun barrel from the raw tubing, a section is cut to length and the ends squared and counterbored slightly. It is then chucked in the lathe at about the midway point and the tailstock center placed in the protruding end. The shank is turned to size and threaded to screw into the extension, or the receiver as the case may be. A straight cylinder some 2 inches long and turned just enough to assure concentricity is left just ahead of the threaded section. If a threaded forend retaining nut is to be used as on the trap barrel shown, a raised band is left at a point 10 1/2 inches forward from the breech end. This band is 1.065 inch in diameter and .625 inch long and threaded 24 threads per inch. The portion between the cylindrical breech section and this threaded band should be turned to a diameter of .950 inch, with the diameter just ahead of the breech section gradually tapered for a distance of some 2 inches and blended into the .950-inch diameter.

The blank is then removed from the lathe, turned end for end, and again chucked with the unturned portion extending from the chuck and the tail stock center supporting the end. If the muzzle brake is to be installed, two bands are left as shown in the drawing and the remainder turned to .900 inch both between the threaded bands and extending back to the forend retainer nut band.

If the assault-type barrel is used, it is made in the same way, except that no threaded bands are required. You should also make sure that the barrel exceeds the legal minimum length of 18 inches enough so that no one will question its legality. There are people who don't know where to begin when it comes to measuring shotgun barrels. Once, several years ago, a bumbling Oklahoma town marshall tried to confiscate one of my box-magazine autoloading guns because, he said, the barrel was too short. He was trying to measure it from the receiver forward. While I was trying to tell him that the barrel extended another five eighths of an inch into the receiver, he insisted that it started at the front edge of the receiver and was illegal. This happened at a small town gun show. Luckily, a state trooper who knew something about guns came along and set him straight. But it could happen again. And to you.

A standard finish reamer can be used to cut the chamber if a pilot bushing that will just enter the bore is fitted to it. If a reamer with a removable pilot bushing is used, you simply make up a larger bushing. If you have a reamer with a solid pilot, you must turn the pilot down enough to make and fit a bushing to it. A carbide lathe tool is used to turn it to .625 inch, and the bushing is bored to just fit over it and turned on the outside to just slip into the bore.

The muzzle end of the barrel is secured in the lathe chuck and the tail stock center inserted in the breech end. The steady rest is mounted on the lathe bed and set up just behind the threaded breech end. If no steady rest is available, the cylindrical breech portion can be caught in the chuck with the muzzle end extending through the headstock. While not actually as important as with a rifle barrel, it is imperative that the bore is centered with as little run out as possible.

Now, with the lathe set up to turn at its lowest speed, the chamber reamer pilot is started in the bore. A tap wrench is secured on the drive end of the reamer with the tailstock center contacting the center hole in the drive end. The pilot and flutes are given a good shot of cutting oil, the lathe turned on, and the reamer fed into the bore by pressure from the tailstock. The tailstock is fed with one hand while the other holds the tap wrench handle to prevent it from turning. Since only a small amount of metal is removed in cutting the chamber, the finish reamer can be used for the entire operation. However, it should be withdrawn frequently and the accumulated chips removed and given a liberal coat of cutting oil.

The rim cut depth, which actually determines headspace, is arrived at by inserting the bolt in its locked position in the barrel extension (or receiver body as the case may be) and measuring from the outside edge of the barrel extension to the bolt face. This measurement will be the same as the distance between the barrel shoulder (which mates against the barrel extension) and the head of a chambered shell or headspace gauge. You should probably subtract .005 to .010 inch from this measurement simply to make sure that a thick-rimmed shell will chamber. A slight amount of excessive headspace is not as critical in a shotgun as many people think. It is far more important that the bolt close and lock on any and all types and makes of factory-loaded shells. Note that I said factory shells. Fully half of these self-styled ballistic geniuses who try to reload ammunition have no idea what they are doing and don't completely resize shells to factory specifications. Therefore, their shells won't chamber in any other gun except the one they were fired in, if that. Chambers must be cut to accommodate factory ammunition only and the reload sized to fit.

With the chamber cut to finished dimensions, the barrel is removed from the lathe and

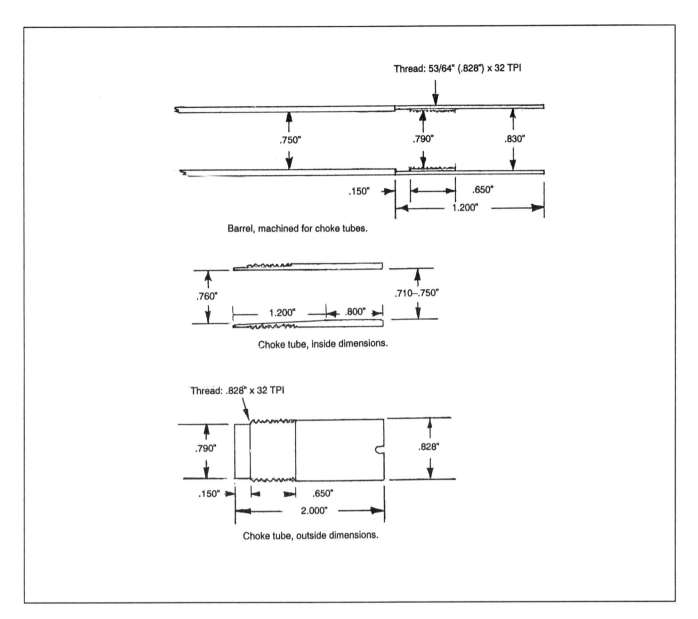

Thread: 53/64" (.828") x 32 TPI

.750"   .790"   .830"

.150"   .650"

1.200"

Barrel, machined for choke tubes.

.760"   .710–.750"

1.200"   .800"

Choke tube, inside dimensions.

Thread: .828" x 32 TPI

.790"   .828"

.150"   .650"

2.000"

Choke tube, outside dimensions.

reversed, whereby the muzzle end is centered in the steady rest or chuck. It is most important here that the bore is centered without runout.

Here again, since we have an oversize bore, no standard tooling is available unless you want to go ahead and install standard-size choke tubes. Even then you will have to make up at least one pilot bushing that just fits the bore and use it on both the reamer and tap.

If several barrels are to be machined to accept the choke tubes, it would be a good idea to either make or have made a suitable reamer and tap with pilots at least 2 inches long to do this work. There are custom tap and reamer makers who will do this work, but they will charge an arm and a leg for it.

If only a few barrels are to be made, and provided the bore runs concentric in the lathe, the machining can be done in the lathe using a boring bar and a small inside threading tool to accommodate the choke tubes shown in the drawing. The inside of the barrel is bored to a diameter of .795 inch and a depth of 2.0 inches at the muzzle end. The first 1.200 inch is then enlarged to .830 inch. These cuts can be made to the exact depth by mounting a dial indicator on the lathe bed and setting it to where the carriage contacts it at a predetermined number, which is the finished depth. The boring tool should be ground at an angle that will form a raised lip at the bottom of the cut. The skirt of the choke tube, when bottomed, then fits inside this lip, and there is no gap between the two to leak gas or for the shot charge to jump.

The smaller diametered portion (the .795 inch part) is threaded 32 threads per inch to a depth of 2.000 inch from the muzzle. Again, this depth can be cut exactly through use of the dial indicator.

Since no standard choke tubes will fit, we will have to make the choke tubes too. While this entails a little bit of extra work, it is worthwhile since we wind up with choke tubes that fit exactly with any choke diameter desired. This is not always possible with commercial chokes.

Seamless tubing is usually available only in 20-foot lengths. If you expect to make up enough choke tubes to make it economical to purchase a full section of this, it comes in a standard size of 7/8 inch (.875 inch) outside diameter, with a wall thickness of .083 inch, leaving an inside bore diameter of .709 inch. This is ideal for our purpose since it only requires turning the outside down .047 inch to a diameter of .828 inch. If you only intend to make a few, it is more economical to obtain a short length of 4130 or 4140 round stock and drill a pilot hole that is enlarged with the boring tool. The only advantage offered by using stainless is that it won't rust in place quite as fast.

A section of the tubing 12 1/4-inch long (this will make six choke tubes) is chucked in the lathe, with enough material extending from the chuck to allow one choke tube to be machined full length. The outside diameter is turned to .828 inch. Use a slightly round nose tool for this and a slow feed to get the finest finish possible. The outside end is turned to .790 inch for a short distance of .150 inch. The next .800 inch is threaded with 32 threads per inch pitch. As the finish thread depth is almost reached, the barrel should be tried on it. Support the chamber end of the barrel with the tail stock center to keep it in line and try to screw the barrel on the choke tube. Keep taking shallow cuts on the choke tube thread until it will just screw on by hand and stop. Of course it would have been easier to try the finished choke tube to the barrel thread while we were cutting it, but we didn't have a choke tube to try.

The inside diameter is bored to size using a boring tool with a long, straight cutting edge. If fed very slowly and using cutting oil, a smooth surface is obtained that, with a bit of polishing,

will be at least the equal of commercial chokes. The rear end, or what might be properly called the "approach cone" portion of the choke tube, can be cut either by setting the compound at one degree and feeding the boring tool with it, or through use of a standard long forcing cone reamer normally used to lengthen the tapered area just ahead of the chamber. If one of the little high-speed hand grinders such as a Dremel tool is available together with the adapter to mount it on the lathe tool post, an extremely smooth finish to the inside of the choke tube can be obtained by using 3/8- or 1/2-inch felt bobs coated with 400 grit buffing compound as a finishing operation.

The finished choke tube is cut to length at the muzzle end, and two or four slots are cut equidistantly around the circumference to enable tightening or removal of the choke tube. A 3/32-inch end mill can be used for this.

The riot gun barrel is made in the same manner except for being shorter. Usually these are used without choke tubes or any choke constriction, resulting simply in a cylinder bore. The muzzle brake can be used or not, as desired. These same methods can be used to make up any other shotgun barrels desired by varying the outside dimensions to suit and changing the barrel thread to mate with whatever action it is used with.

Rifle barrels are turned and fitted using much the same methods. As previously mentioned, you should obtain a barrel blank with all the excess metal possible already removed. If you are required to turn a full-length taper, the easiest way is to set the tail stock over enough to cut the desired taper. It must be turned between centers. The steady rest is adjusted to support the barrel and positioned about halfway between each end. Then, with a slightly round nosed cutting tool fed with a fairly fast feed, the portion between the tail stock and the steady rest is turned to size. The steady rest is loosened and moved toward the chuck and remounted and the exposed portion turned to size. The steady rest is then removed and remounted between the lathe carriage and the tail stock. This allows access for the cutting tool to turn the remainder to size. Barrels turned in this fashion will probably require draw filing after turning to remove tool marks, high and low places along the barrel that show-up as "ripples," or wavy surfaces when sighting along the length of the barrel after polishing and bluing.

Chambering and threading is accomplished in the same manner used for the shotgun barrel except that it is imperative that the bore runs absolutely concentric and true. The steady rest should be used to support the breech end and a short section at the muzzle caught in the chuck.

The chamber should be cut by first using a roughing reamer, which removes the bulk of the excess metal, followed by the finish reamer, which removes only a small amount. Many gunsmiths, in an attempt to save money, buy only a finish reamer and use it to cut the entire chamber. This is poor economy since a reamer used in this fashion will wear and become dull rapidly. If only the finish reamer is available, at least part of the excess metal should be removed with drills that are slightly smaller than the finished chamber diameter, followed by the finish reamer as described. Chambers can be polished using 400 to 600 grit wet or dry sandpaper, followed by crocus cloth wrapped around a small dowel and held against the chamber wall as the barrel revolves.

Chapter
Recoil
10

Recoil can be described as an opposing reaction caused by the pressure required to push a bullet or shot charge up the bore.

When a cartridge or shell is fired, expanding gasses from the ignited powder charge push the projectile up the bore with sometimes as much as 60,000 pounds per square inch of pressure behind it. This pressure expands in all directions, but since it is contained by the chamber walls, it pushes forward against the base of the projectile. At the same time, it is trying to push the gun to the rear with the same amount of pressure, plus an additional amount caused by friction and resistance between the projectile and the bore.

Since the projectile usually weighs less that 2 ounces in the case of the shotgun and usually less than 500 grains in rifles and pistols, and the gun weighs several pounds, the gun moves to the rear far more slowly than the projectile moves up the bore. Therefore, a heavy gun will have less apparent recoil than a lighter one of similar design and caliber.

That at least one of the factors governing perceived recoil rests in the human mind can be illustrated by a couple of incidents that happened several years ago.

A few years back, I had a trap range in conjunction with my gun shop. We usually held a registered shoot about once a month and shot practice rounds and for fun on other weekends.

On one particular weekend, a lady who shot with us regularly came to me and told me she thought the recoil reducer in the buttstock of her Ljutic Mono gun had shifted or turned since the gun seemed to be kicking her more than usual. She asked if I would look and see if that was what was wrong.

I took it into the shop and removed the recoil pad. There was no recoil reducer in the stock. Not even a hole for one.

As an experiment, I put the recoil pad back on her gun and took it back to her. I told her that it was, indeed, turned wrong. She proceeded to shoot the gun the rest of the afternoon and insisted that it didn't kick nearly as

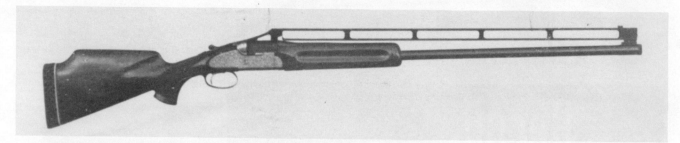

This high-rib Weatherby conversion cut recoil by at least 20 percent.

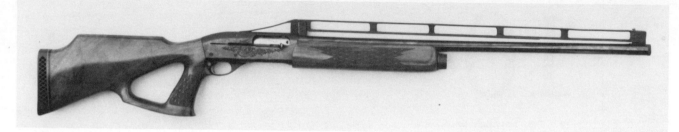

This high sight line Remington 1100 has less recoil than before.

A straight-line recoil with a high sight line lessens felt recoil, especially to the facial area.

much as it did before. When she had finished shooting for the day, I took her and the gun into my shop and again removed the recoil pad. When I showed her that the gun had never even been bored to accommodate a recoil reducer, she became quite angry, insisting that she had paid the people who sold her the gun an exorbitant price to install one. I installed one for her. And while I personally couldn't tell any difference either before or after the installation, she insisted that it cut the recoil of the gun in half.

During this same time period I had a M870 Remington slide-action trap gun for which I had installed a gas-operated recoil reducer of my own design in the magazine tube. I asked a squad of shooters to shoot their five rounds each on one station with this gun. All five agreed that the gun had considerably less recoil than a similar gun without the device.

I took the gun back into the shop, and a short time later, brought it back out to the same five shooters. I told them that this gun had a heavier weight in the recoil device and a larger gas port

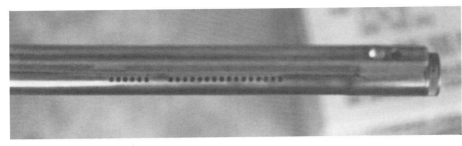

"Porting" may lessen muzzle jump but does little to lessen recoil (left).

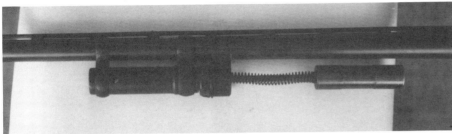

The piston assembly used in that shotgun (left).

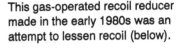

This gas-operated recoil reducer made in the early 1980s was an attempt to lessen recoil (below).

and asked them to shoot this one and give me their thoughts on which one kicked the most.

To my surprise, three of the shooters said this one kicked less, one said more, and the other one just grinned. I never did tell them it was the same gun.

So as you can see, it is possible to convince many shooters that a gun has less recoil than it actually has without really doing anything to reduce it. There are, however, several ways to actually reduce recoil considerably.

Probably the easiest way is to simply install one or two of the so called "recoil reducers" in the buttstock. The main reason that these may seem to reduce recoil is due to the added weight, which a handful of rocks would do just as well. However, as illustrated previously, the knowledge that they are there will convince many shooters that the gun actually kicks less.

A straight line stock with a high sighting plane on the order of the M16 military rifle will reduce perceived recoil somewhat. Actually the gun will still generate approximately the same amount of recoil as a conventional firearm of the same weight and caliber. The high sight line allows the shooter to shoot with his/her head

erect, and the straight line design causes recoil to be directed straight back into the shoulder instead of upward into the cheek. There is also little or no muzzle jump or rise with a design of this type. This will also tend to convince the shooter that the gun has less recoil than the conventional design.

Various spring-loaded or hydraulically dampened telescoping buttstocks have been tried. Probably the best of these was one called a Hydracoil stock. It had a hydraulic cylinder to absorb recoil and was quite effective. Winchester sold Model 12s so equipped. For some reason, probably because most were made of plastic, they didn't sell well and more or less faded away. Just in the last few years these stocks have been "rediscovered," and while most are effective, they are also ugly. Most have a strut or cylinder or two protruding from the butt end of the stock with a recoil pad mounted on the end, leaving a gap at least an inch wide between the end of the stock and the recoil pad. This may be effective, but it looks terrible, which is probably the reason most shooters don't use them.

Some time ago I designed one to use on my trap gun. This one has the spring-loaded cylin-

A 12-gauge, bolt-action, single-shot trap gun with muzzle brake and spring-loaded, telescoping buttstock. It has very little perceived recoil.

A 12-gauge, slide-action, box-magazine shotgun with muzzle brake.

der fastened to the receiver of the gun with the buttstock surrounding it. It still isn't pretty, but it has fairly clean lines without any open gaps. This one absorbs more recoil than any of the others that I have tried. A description of how to make these is included in Chapter 14.

It is possible, in the case of the shotgun, to increase the bore diameter from .005 inch to .050 inch over the accepted standard size. This results in less friction, with a corresponding decrease in recoil. This can be overdone to a point where wads no longer seal,. especially in cold weather. From my own experience, I believe some .020 inch over standard is probably best. It has been said that lengthening the forcing cone to 1 3/8 or 1 1/2 inch reduces recoil substantially. It doesn't really do all that much, but if the shooter thinks it does, why not?

Another school of thought has produced the idea that porting the shotgun barrel by drilling one or more rows of small holes on each side of the rib and just behind the choke reduces recoil. This is seen mostly on single-barrel trap guns and is touted as reducing muzzle jump. It doesn't reduce recoil much, if any. And with a singles

gun where a rapid second shot is uncalled for, who gives a damn if the muzzle jumps. With a straight line design, it won't jump anyway.

The most effective recoil-reduction device that can be fitted to rifles, shotguns, and some pistols is the muzzle brake. One of these, properly designed, can reduce recoil more than any other known device.

The muzzle brake designs shown in Chapter 11 are effective and do not increase the noise level significantly. Keep in mind that the larger the diameter of the expansion chamber, the more effective the brake will be.

If we design a rifle or shotgun using the high sight line and straight line design with a telescoping buttstock and an efficient muzzle brake combined with the bore modifications previously mentioned (in the case of the shotgun), the end result probably won't be as graceful as some, but it will most assuredly result in a firearm with less recoil than ever before experienced. This is especially desirable in a trap gun, where the shooter may shoot some 200 to 300 rounds in a single day. It also makes heavy caliber rifles pleasant to shoot.

Muzzle Brakes

11

The most effective means of recoil reduction is the muzzle brake. Properly designed and installed, these can actually eliminate as much as 80 percent of felt recoil. The drawbacks inherent with the use of these are, in most cases, an increase in the noise level. A really effective brake will increase the noise level somewhat, regardless of what some people may tell you about "quiet" muzzle brakes. They also add some to the girth and sometimes length at the muzzle.

A really effective brake will be some 2 inches long when installed on a rifle barrel, around 6 inches long on a shotgun, and anywhere from 1 to 2 inches on a pistol. The diameter should be the largest possible without interfering with the sight picture. For maximum effectiveness, the shotgun brake should be at least 1 1/2 inch in diameter. This makes a high sight line almost mandatory. Diameter of the rifle brake can be from .600 inch for calibers .30 or smaller if installed on conventional stocked rifles to as much as an inch if used on a high sight line gun.

Here again, efficiency will improve as the diameter is increased. Pistol brakes can, in many instances, be machined directly into the barrel without any increase in length or diameter.

The inside diameter is bored and threaded at the rear end to screw onto the correspondingly threaded muzzle end of the barrel. The remaining body is bored leaving a wall thickness of .050 to .060 inch, the wall at the forward end some .100 to .125 inch thick, and an exit hole .004 to .008 inch larger than the bullet diameter.

Gas exit holes are indexed and drilled perpendicular to the bore and should conform to a regular pattern, mostly for the sake of appearance. These can be round holes of .187 inch diameter, spaced .300 inch apart, and laid out in six or eight rows of four holes each spaced equidistantly around the diameter.

The shotgun brake will require six or eight rows of .125 inch holes spaced .200 inch apart in rows approximately 4 inches long. The inside of the barrel must be polished after drilling to

A tapered muzzle brake mounted on a trap gun. The front sight is adjustable for both windage and elevation (above).

The completed shotgun muzzle brake (right).

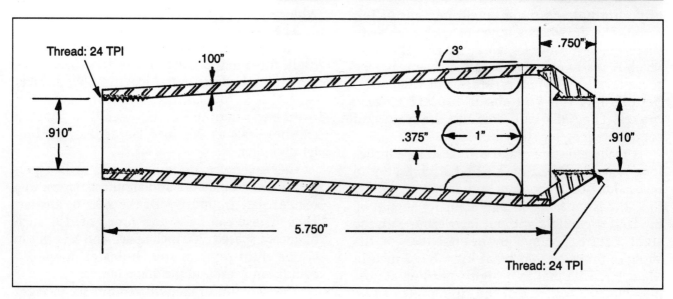

Shotgun muzzle brake with tapered body.

Threading the muzzle brake.

Ports are drilled in the barrel using the milling machine.

The pilot hole is drilled through the brake body.

Outside diameter is turned to size.

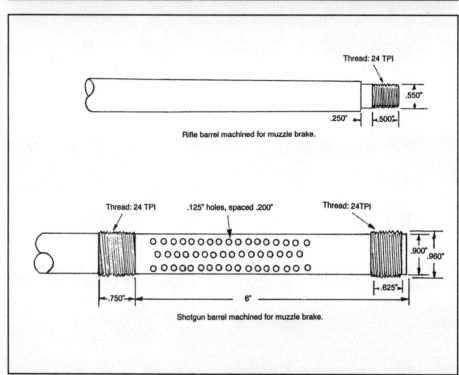

Thread: 24 TPI

.550"

.250" .500"

Rifle barrel machined for muzzle brake.

Thread: 24 TPI   .125" holes, spaced .200"   Thread: 24TPI

.900" .960"

.750"   6"   .625"

Shotgun barrel machined for muzzle brake.

remove any burrs or cratering incurred during drilling. Needless to say, these holes are located behind the choke.

The muzzle end of the barrel must be threaded, 24 threads per inch, and a raised collar must be located 6 inches to the rear of the muzzle. If the barrel is turned from an oversize blank, a length five eighths of an inch long and enough oversize to thread should be left just behind the muzzle and another of similar dimensions 6 inches behind the muzzle. If using a barrel that is already too small for this, it will be necessary to make collars, bored to a slip fit over the barrel, and silver solder them in place.

The muzzle brake body is made of aluminum, in this installation, to save weight. If possible, it should be 1 3/4 inch in diameter at the muzzle end and bored to a .100-inch wall thickness.

If the tapered version is used, which looks better than the straight cylinder, the rear end should be bored to size and threaded first. It is then screwed onto a short dummy barrel section that has been correspondingly threaded. The

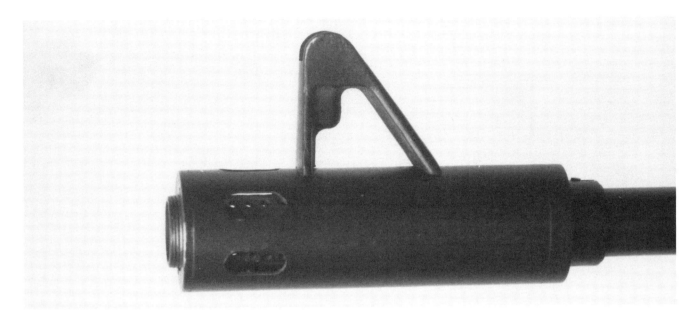

Muzzle brake mounted on 12-gauge, slide-action gun

dummy barrel, or arbor, can then be chucked in the lathe and the taper cut using the compound slide set at the proper angle. If using a small lathe with less than sufficient travel on the compound, you will have to cut the taper in two setups, cutting to the limit of the compound travel, then moving the carriage enough to cut the rest.

A plug, or cap, is turned to fit into the front end and threaded to screw onto the barrel.

Gas ports should be a series of 3/8-inch slots, 1 inch long, spaced equidistantly around the diameter and just to the rear of the muzzle cap.

A straight cylinder brake is made in the same manner, except that no taper is cut, either inside or out, and an end plug similar to the muzzle cap must be used at the back end also.

A sleeve, or jam nut, is bored and threaded to screw onto the collar at the rear end of the brake. A couple of .187-inch holes are drilled through the sides to allow tightening with a spanner wrench. In use, this collar is threaded on to the barrel first, followed by the brake body, then the end cap. With the front sight, or rib post, in its desired position, the collar is drawn up against the rear end of the brake, locking it in place. It is

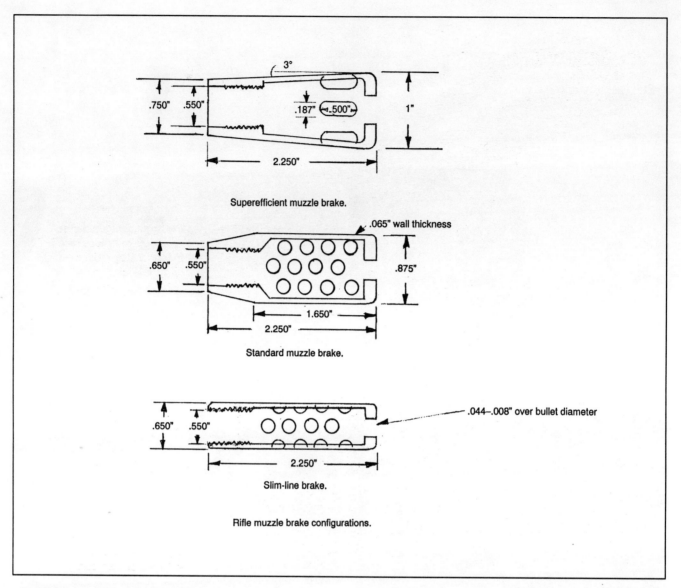

Superefficient muzzle brake.

Standard muzzle brake.

Slim-line brake.

Rifle muzzle brake configurations.

possible to make lateral adjustments for windage by rotating the brake body before tightening.

The front sight or rib post should be fabricated and fastened in place on the brake body. While it is possible to weld it in place, I recommend that it be held in place using screws unless you are a bona fide expert at welding aluminum. Welding thin aluminum parts is a tricky business, and you can easily wind up with ruined parts if this is attempted.

Another drawback to using aluminum is the fact that it can't be blued by conventional methods. It will require anodizing, which is an expensive process to set up for. Unless you can find a commercial metal finisher offering this process, the only other choice is to paint it.

In the event you are compelled to do this, the metal surfaces should be bead blasted or sand blasted first to give a slightly rough finish for the paint to adhere to. A thin coat of flat black enamel is sprayed on and allowed to dry, followed by a second coat. When thoroughly dry, it is then placed in an oven and baked at 350 to 400 degrees for a couple of hours. This results in a fairly durable finish and, if properly done, will look almost as good as a commercial finish.

The larger-than-bore-diameter expansion chamber, with a wall at the front end for the gasses to push against, is the key element to an efficient muzzle brake. When a comparison is made, the ones having a hole through the body just slightly larger than bore diameter and forward-sloping gas ports are sadly lacking.

When installing the rifle brake, the barrel should be threaded between centers and the threads cut with as little slack as possible. It is

Porting a shotgun barrel does little to reduce recoil, though it may reduce muzzle jump. Gun design will achieve the same result.

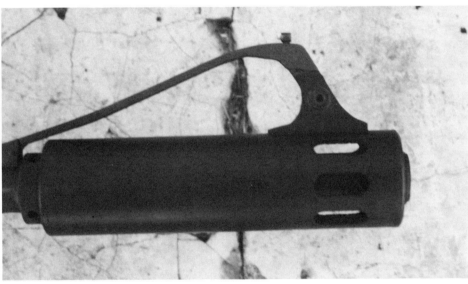

Cylindrical muzzle brake on a 12-gauge trap gun.

Threaded arbor is mounted in lathe chuck. The brake is screwed onto it for outside finish cuts.

Standard muzzle brake mounted on arbor.

Tapered muzzle brake mounted on arbor.

Muzzle Brakes 79

essential that the bullet exit hole be concentric with the bore. Otherwise accuracy will suffer.

Be warned that inexperienced federal agents may very well try to seize shotguns equipped with the muzzle brakes described here. On more than one occasion in the past, they have mistaken them for silencers. There is no reason to believe that they are any smarter now than they were then.

Chapter

Trigger Assemblies

12

Trigger assemblies, as described here, will include the trigger, hammer, sear, disconnector, trigger bar, and whatever springs are required. It is recommended that these parts be housed in a separate housing contained inside the frame, or receiver, that can be removed and installed as a unit. This not only eliminates unsightly exposed pins, it also blocks each end of the pins and holds them in place.

I have included sketches of 12 different trigger assemblies. One of these should fit any design requirements called for. There are at least 20 more that could be included, but it would require a separate book to describe them all.

As you design your mechanism, keep in mind that spring and pin locations can have an effect on the finished product. If the trigger spring is placed 1/2 inch from the pivot pin, for example, it will have slightly less pressure but will be far easier to compress than if the spring is only 1/4 inch from the pin. If the portion of the trigger that actuates, or bears against, the sear or hammer is 1/2 inch above the pivot pin,

it will take twice as much effort to pull than if it is 1/4 inch away. However, the trigger will require twice as much movement to fire the gun. When a trigger bar is used to push or pull the sear out of engagement, the pivot pin that locates the trigger bar should have as much distance between it and the trigger pivot pin as possible. This reduces trigger travel in direct proportion to the distance between the two pins.

In designs incorporating a safety, if it really is a safety, it will lock the sear securely into the hammer notch. Do not try to get by with a safety that only blocks the trigger. These give a false sense of security since the sear can be jarred or vibrated out of contact with the hammer, especially if dropped. Don't take chances with this.

Sketch number one shows what is likely the simplest trigger mechanism known since the matchlock. There are only two moving parts. The trigger nose engages in a notch in the hammer, holding it in the cocked position until the trigger is pulled. Since there is no disconnector, the hammer is free to move forward any time the trigger

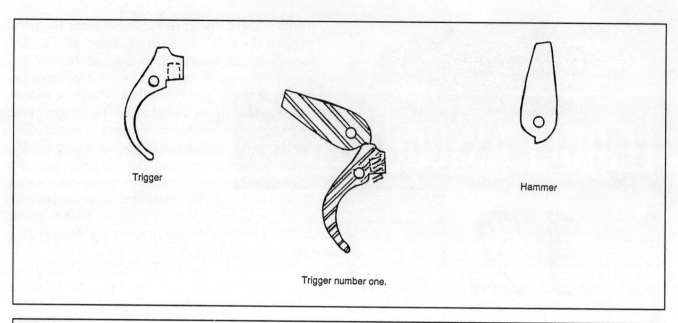

Trigger

Hammer

Trigger number one.

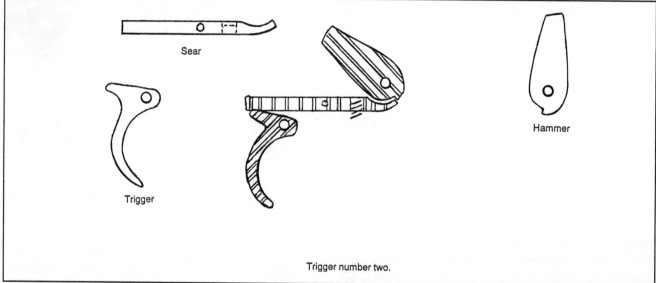

Sear

Trigger

Hammer

Trigger number two.

is depressed. This assembly is useful primarily in single shots and single-action revolvers.

Number two is similar to number one except that a sear bar is added. While this is done primarily so that the trigger can be positioned further to the rear in relation to the hammer, it is also possible to obtain an easier trigger pull since the camming lever portion of the trigger will have more leverage. If the hammer notch and the sear nose are smooth and square, a fairly good trigger pull can be obtained. Since no disconnector is provided here either, this one is also better suited to single shots.

Number three is useful when the trigger must be positioned a distance in front of the hammer. A trigger bar and disconnector are added here,

making this assembly adaptable for use in reciprocating bolt actions. The sear engages a slot in the top of the hammer, holding it in the cocked position. Rearward movement of the trigger bar pushes the sear out of engagement. Movement to the rear of the bolt rides the disconnector downward, camming the trigger bar out of engagement with the sear. The disconnector should be close to the rear edge of the bolt, preventing discharge until the bolt is fully locked.

Number four is similar to number three, except the trigger is located behind the hammer. It can be located whatever distance behind that is required simply by extending the length of the trigger bar and disconnector. A separate disconnector is used. If made on the trigger bar, as in

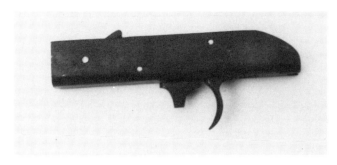

Removable trigger assembly for pistol.

Shotgun trigger assembly.

number three, the forward movement required to push the sear out of engagement would also move the disconnector into the rear edge of the bolt, camming the trigger bar out of engagement. Since a considerable distance exists between the trigger bar pin and the trigger pivot pin, very little trigger movement is required to fire the gun. A sliding safety is used here which, when pushed to the rear, locks the sear into the face of the hammer. The only way anyone could make this one fire with the safety engaged would be to exert enough pressure on it to break it. The safety is disengaged by pushing it forward with the trigger finger.

Number five is used in striker-fired guns such as bolt actions. It works in much the same way as a M70 Winchester trigger except the sear is reversed since it is necessary to move the trigger forward in relation to the rear end of the bolt. I have used this trigger design in my bolt-action trap guns. With the sear stoned smooth and square and the trigger notch to match, a safe

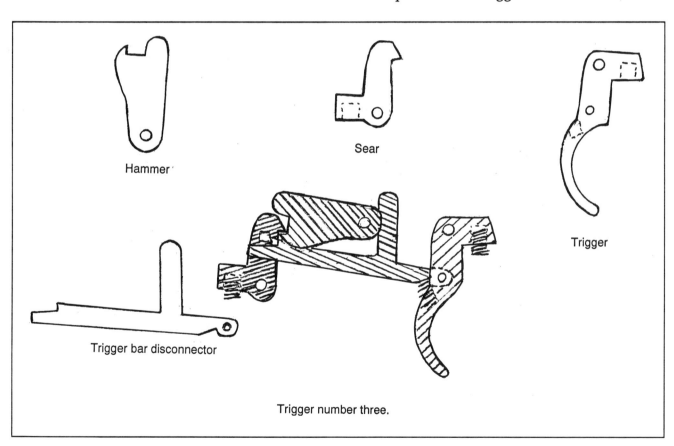

Hammer

Sear

Trigger

Trigger bar disconnector

Trigger number three.

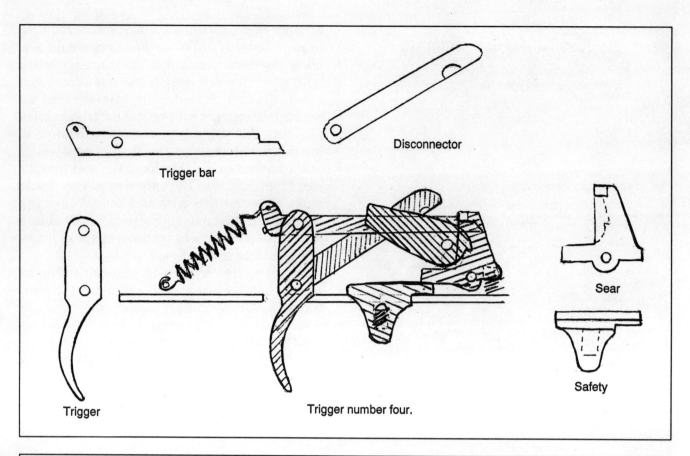

Trigger bar

Disconnector

Sear

Safety

Trigger

Trigger number four.

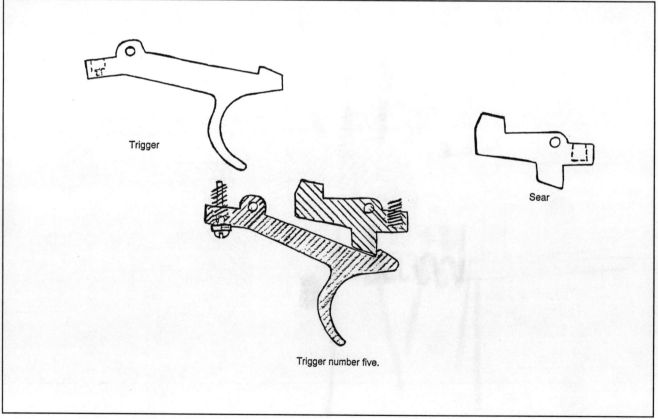

Trigger

Sear

Trigger number five.

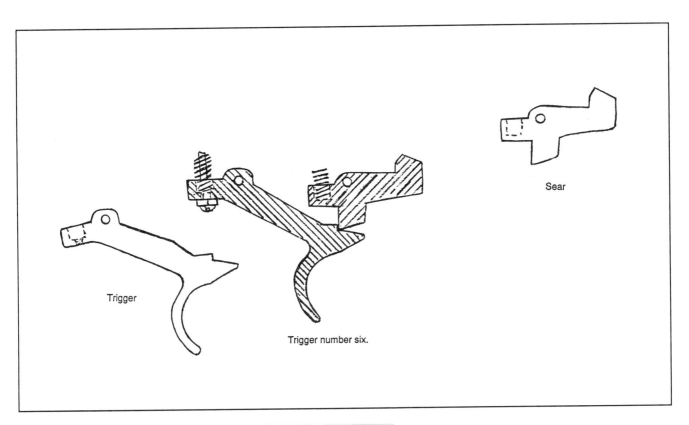

Trigger

Trigger number six.

Sear

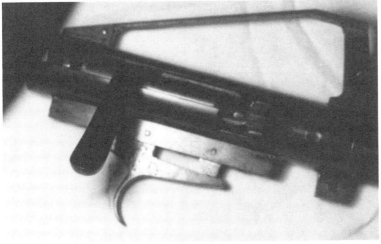

This trigger assembly for a single-shot shotgun is similar to the Winchester M70 trigger. It provides a safe, light pull with very little trigger movement. This is desirable in a shotgun.

Perazzi release trigger conversion made by the author.

2-pound trigger with very little movement can be obtained. There are people who think such a trigger is not necessary on a shotgun, but anyone who ever tried one liked it. The screw behind the trigger pivot pin serves as a guide for the trigger spring and eliminates overtravel. This is an excellent bolt-action trigger.

Number six works in the same way, except that the sear is turned around, resembling the M70 trigger closely. This design permits the trigger to be moved further to the rear than number five. If these are used in a trap gun or single-shot target rifle, a safety is of little concern. If used in a magazine gun or a hunting type, a safety should be incorporated. It can be installed directly in front of the trigger, whereby pushing it to the rear locks the trigger to the sear. It is pushed forward to disengage. The same safety design will work on number five equally well.

Number seven is another for use in striker-fired guns. In this case the sear drops straight down when the trigger pulls the drawbar-type sear from under it. This trigger is especially useful when you need a trigger positioned still further to the rear. It is slightly harder to manufacture than numbers five and six but it is

very positive and can be set up to give a very light pull with little trigger movement. This one will require a lever or crossbolt safety just behind the trigger, which will prevent any rearward movement when engaged.

Number eight is a very simple trigger for use in striker-fired guns. It can be set up with a light pull and probably the least amount of movement as any described. This one, too, can have the sliding safety just ahead of the trigger.

Number nine is a release trigger for a striker-fired gun. There are any number of trap shooters who believe they simply must have a release trigger. To those not familiar with the term, a release trigger is exactly as it is named—the shooter pulls the trigger to the rear and holds it until the instant of firing, at which time he simply relaxes the rearward pressure, *releasing* it, and the gun fires. Many shooters use these believing that they prevent flinching. Others think they are faster than a pull trigger. This may or may not be true. But if the shooter thinks it is, and it helps him, why not?

Such a trigger has little value for use in hunting weapons and could be dangerous. But in the trap gun, where the shooter has all the time he

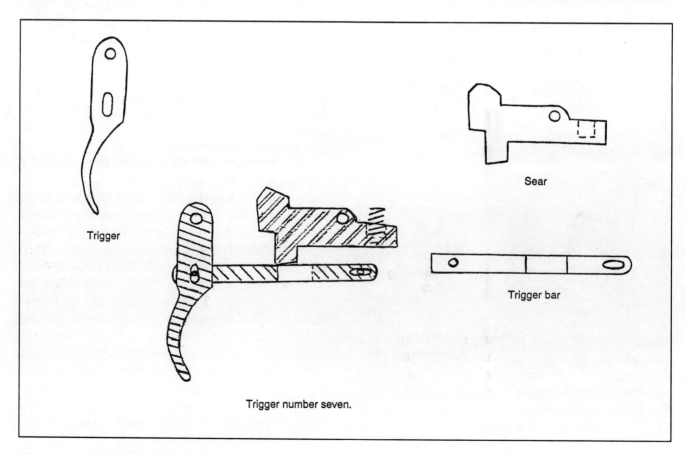

Trigger

Sear

Trigger bar

Trigger number seven.

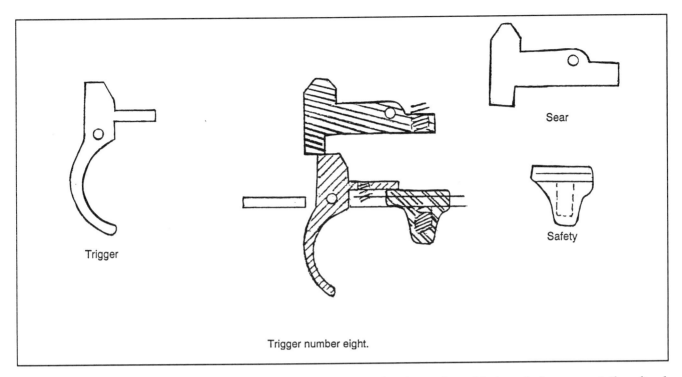

Trigger

Sear

Safety

Trigger number eight.

Shotgun trigger parts.

A release trigger conversion.

er-fired gun, but this is only because striker-fired trap guns are virtually nonexistent.

A few years ago I made up several sniper rifles, both in medium and longer range. These were bolt-action guns, and I had used the number six trigger in the design. I had been planning to build a bolt-action trap gun so I designed a release trigger for it and went ahead and put one in one of the rifles. I asked the people who were getting the guns to try it and tell me how they liked it. I didn't hear anything for several weeks. But then, one day they brought back all the guns that I had delivered and wanted a similar trigger installed in each one.

These triggers set with somewhere around a 5-pound pull and require very little pressure to hold. Simply relaxing the trigger finger causes the gun to fire, and the shooter already has any flinching that he might be guilty of over when he pulls the trigger. I would imagine these would be popular on target rifles if publicized.

Number ten is also a release trigger for the striker-fired gun. This one has a sliding drawbar to serve as a secondary sear and activate the primary sear. It should be used when it is necessary to move the trigger further forward or to the rear, since the trigger proper can be moved along the lower face of the drawbar. Either of these triggers can be converted to pull triggers by turning in the screw located on the

needs to position the gun and set his trigger, it can be quite useful. It also has merit when used in certain target or sniper rifles. Again, the shooter must have ample time to set the trigger before firing. Frankly, I have never known of anyone else making a release trigger for a strik-

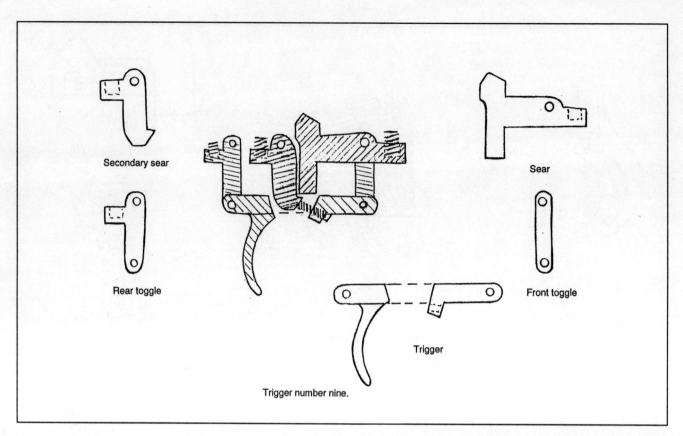

Secondary sear

Rear toggle

Sear

Front toggle

Trigger

Trigger number nine.

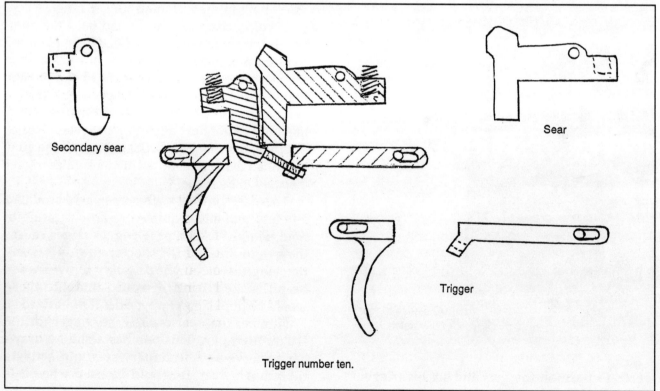

Secondary sear

Sear

Trigger

Trigger number ten.

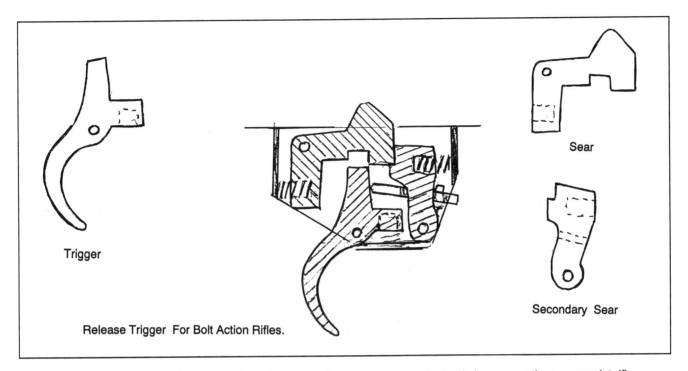

Trigger

Release Trigger For Bolt Action Rifles.

Sear

Secondary Sear

This release trigger is adaptable to striker-fired, bolt-action firearms. It is most desirable in target, sniper, or varmint rifles where deliberate shots are the rule. In use, when the trigger is pulled or moved to the rear, the upper front edge of the trigger moves forward, blocking the sear. At the same time, it moves the secondary sear forward out of engagement with the sear. This allows the sear to move slightly downward, preventing reengagement of the secondary sear. Thus, when pressure on the trigger is relaxed, the sear moves out of engagement with the firing pin, allowing it to move forward and fire the cartridge. This permits an especially "fast" trigger, with most opportunity to flinch removed.

bottom of the sear bar. This will cause the sear to be pushed out of engagement before the secondary sear engages, causing the firing pin to go forward when the trigger is pulled. Backing off this screw a couple of turns will allow the sear bar to be pulled under the sear block before the primary sear releases. This blocks the sear block and keeps it from falling when the trigger is pulled further to the rear, releasing the primary sear. When the trigger is allowed to move forward, the sear bar also moves forward and out from under the sear block, allowing it to fall and the firing pin to move forward, firing the gun.

Number eleven is a release trigger for hammer-fired guns. These are the type usually found in break-open single and over/under trap guns. I have also used them in my own hammer-fired guns. These are easier to make than numbers nine and ten. This is primarily a trigger of the number two design with a pin placed through the side of the hammer, with one end protruding from the right side. A secondary sear is made from 1/8-inch flat stock with a tab folded over at

the tail end to contact the upper side of the trigger at the rear end. An adjustment screw is installed in the cam portion of the trigger to bear against this tab. In use, the adjustment screw is turned in to a point that it cams the hook end of the primary sear over the hammer pin just before the primary sear releases the hammer. As the hammer is released, it moves forward slightly until arrested by the hook over the pin. When pressure on the trigger is relaxed, the hook no longer bears on the pin, thereby permitting the hammer to move forward. Backing the screw out a couple of turns will disengage the secondary sear, allowing the assembly to operate as a standard pull trigger.

When the trigger begins to "pull through" or fire when the trigger is pulled, the adjustment screw is turned in slightly, which moves the secondary sear forward, restoring its release trigger function.

In use, the release trigger must be dependable. It must not fire prematurely or when the trigger is pulled. A good test for proper adjustment can be made by placing one thumb against

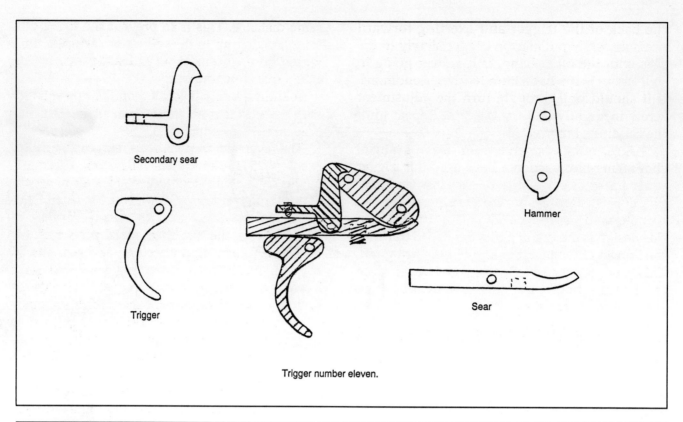

Secondary sear

Hammer

Trigger

Sear

Trigger number eleven.

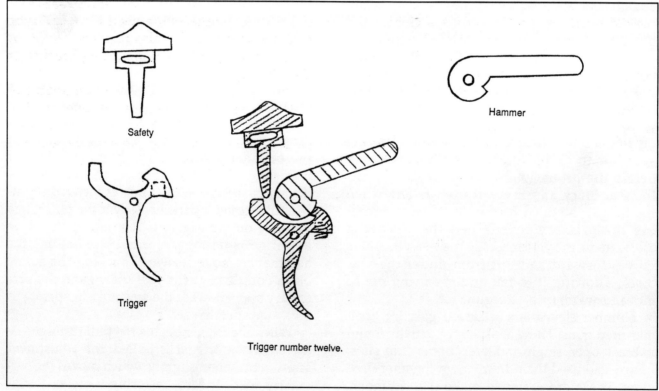

Safety

Hammer

Trigger

Trigger number twelve.

the back of the trigger and exerting forward pressure while pulling the trigger slowly to the rear with the other hand. If it is ever going to pull through, it will do it under these conditions. If it should pull through, turn the adjustment screw in slightly and try it again. Repeat until the condition is corrected.

Trigger number twelve is for use in a single-shot falling-block action. I have used this trigger in several guns of my own design. It is very simple, consisting of only two moving parts: the hammer and the trigger. The main drawback to this design is the use of a transfer bar to transmit the impact of the hammer blow to the firing pin. This is not unique to this design, however, since most such actions use a similar system of some sort. This one uses less parts.

When the operating lever is depressed, it draws the breechblock down with it. The rear edge of the breechblock contacts the front face of the hammer, forcing it downward against the spring until the hammer notch rotates far enough downward to permit the trigger to engage the hammer notch and hold it in the cocked position. As the action is closed, the breechblock moves upward. When the trigger is pulled, the hammer moves to the top, striking the lower rear leg of the transfer bar, which drives the vertical leg into the firing pin, moving it forward into the primer. The hammer is stopped by the rear end of the breechblock, while the inertia firing pin continues to travel another .040 inch forward and rebounds the

same distance. This is to prevent the firing pin from hanging up in the primer or cartridge rim, which could break it or at least prevent the action from opening freely.

A sliding safety is located on the upper tang, with a leg that contacts the rear of the trigger, preventing movement.

The hammers, triggers, sears, etc., can be made from 1/4-, 5/16-, and 3/8-inch flat stock. This must be quality material that will stand a lot of shock and contain enough carbon to heat treat. The annealed flat spring stock is also suitable for this.

If possible, the thin sheet metal parts such as the trigger bars, disconnectors, and secondary sears should be made from this same material. There is a good chance that you won't be able to find any. You can either cut the thicker material down to the appropriate thickness with the milling machine, or you can make them from 12-gauge sheet metal and case harden them.

The trigger housings, when used, can be bent to shape from 16-gauge sheet metal. In several of these designs, mousetrap-type springs such as M16 hammer springs are used for the same purpose. This eliminates the need for a coil-type hammer spring, which also requires a strut, or guide, and sometimes a mounting bracket. It also saves space.

Parts made from 4140 should be heated to 1500 to 1600 degrees Fahrenheit, quenched in oil, and drawn at 800 degrees. Flat spring stock parts are quenched at 1450 to 1550 degrees and drawn at 600 degrees.

Chapter

Magazines

13

The primary key to flawless operation of a multishot firearm lies in the use of a sturdy, properly designed magazine. A magazine should retain its shape, have lips that won't spring or bend, and feed the top cartridge in the same plane regardless of whether the magazine is fully loaded, half full, or down to the last round.

Since a close fit between the magazine and magazine housing (or well, or whatever it is called on your particular gun) is an absolute requirement to assure flawless feeding, the magazine should be built or otherwise acquired first and the gun designed around it. If possible, I suggest that you buy magazines that are already in existence, provided that high-quality magazines can be obtained. Otherwise you will have to make them yourself. While this may seem impossible, it isn't really all that difficult, only time consuming.

Again, one should buy commercial magazines and adapt them to his use. Today it is possible to purchase satisfactory magazines to handle .22 rimfire, 9mm, .223, .308, and some-

times .45, as well as several others. Several weeks ago a company gave me several 10-shot 12-gauge plastic magazines. I made up a gun to use them (the plastic is thicker than sheet metal and requires a larger magazine housing) and they seem to work all right. I don't know how long they will last; probably not as long as metal ones. But one could certainly save a lot of work by using these in building a shotgun.

It is possible to purchase new British Sten 9mm magazines for $3 to $5. The only complaint I have with these is they advertise them either blued or parkerized. If you order the blued, you get magazines painted black. If you order parkerized, you get magazines painted grey. In either case, the paint must be stripped off and the metal refinished for them to look right.

These Sten magazines are quite versatile. I have reshaped their lips and followers to make them high capacity and fit inside angled pistol grips. I have swaged the inside longer so they would hold 20 .45 ACP rounds. By widening the lips slightly, they will feed 10mm ammo. I have

Commercial magazines made for use in the Thompson .22 were used in my MP22 pistols (above).

Straight-bodied magazines such as this will not feed when fully loaded in shotguns (above right).

Sten magazines—shown here in an AR-15/M16 conversion—can be shortened to 15-round capacity, resulting in a more compact weapon (right).

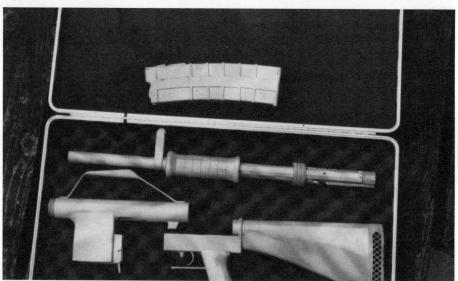

cut them off and bent new flanges at the bottom to remount the bottom plate, making 15-round capacity jobs that interchanged with the full-length ones. I used these for years in my MP83 assault pistols in all three calibers. There are numerous others currently manufactured for other guns that could be used. The only advantage they offer is a considerably higher price.

Whatever kind you use, or if you make it yourself, it should be a single-row feed type, not one that feeds from each side of a double row of cartridges. These are the ones that are most likely to cause jams.

For several years I used what Numrich and later Gun Parts Inc. call a "universal" magazine. These have a capacity of 30 to 32 rounds, depending on who is counting. The first batch I got were junk, with lips so thin and soft I had to rebend them after every few shots. And no two were exactly the same size. They had to be individually fitted to one gun. This caused me all sorts of grief, especially when one person bought more than one gun and managed to get the magazines mixed up. But they got better. The last shipment I got worked perfectly, far better than the thick, clumsy plastic magazines that some of the manufacturers that copied my guns are using. The major drawback to these is they are deeply curved, which eliminates their use in a grip-housed design. There are others of 20-round capacity that can be used for this purpose.

.223 and .308 magazines are available as military surplus. So are .30/06 and numerous others. Gun Parts Inc. even lists Spanish American War

Plastic magazines save a lot of work but probably won't last as long as metal.

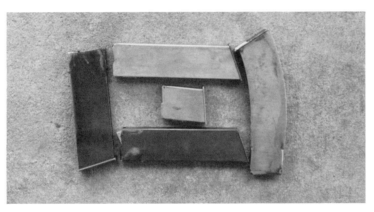

Several experimental magazines made by the author.

surplus Remington Lee .45/70 magazines for sale. So it is very likely that a magazine is available that can be incorporated into your project.

There are times and situations, though, where the only way to come up with a suitable magazine is to make it yourself. It is recommended that slightly heavier metal than is used in commercial products be used in the construction of such magazines. Many of these are made from 26- to 24-gauge material, which is only .0179 to .0239 inch in thickness. The ones we make will use 20 gauge, which is .0359 inch or, for all practical purposes, .036 inch thick, or 21 gauge for smaller magazines, which is .0329 inch, or .033 inch, thick. The end result will weight slightly more but will be stronger and resist bending or deforming far more than the thinner ones.

It would be ideal if you can obtain sheet metal with enough carbon in it to permit heat treatment whereby some springy action is obtained. Try to get whatever metal you use in a cold-rolled finish as opposed to hot rolled. This is done primarily because the cold rolled already has a fairly good surface finish, which makes the final finishing much easier. Also, many times the hot-rolled material has imperfections or inclusions rolled into it which may not show up until polishing is done, and which may very well render the part useless. Shim stock is available from machine tool supply companies in a thickness of .031 inch and widths up to 6 inches. It is also possible to obtain oil-hardening flat stock in 1/32 or .03125 inch thickness and up to 6 inches wide from the same source. They will charge you almost as much for this material as they would for pure silver.

Chances are, you will go to a sheet metal shop and buy your material there. As mentioned before, try to obtain cold-finished material. This may very well work out better anyway, since this material can be bent or folded to sharp angles without as much danger of splitting or cracking as is present with the use of material with higher carbon content.

If only a few magazines are to be made, usually they can be bent around a form block. Otherwise, makeshift forming dies should be made.

When a form block is made, it should reflect the inside dimensions of the magazine to be formed. An example is a double-row, single-feed 9mm magazine with a 30-round capacity. The inside width should be .740 to .750 inch and the inside length a minimum of 1.250 inch. So the form block can be easily made from a 10-inch long piece of 3/4 by 1 1/4-inch bar stock. The front edges should be rounded to a 1/8 inch, or thereabout, radius. This can be ground, filed, or cut with the milling machine if a corner rounding end mill, or radius cutter as some call it, is available. An equal taper is cut on each side at the top. The taper begins 1 1/8 inch below the top and reduces the width of .750 to .400 inch at the top. The angle is approximately 5 degrees. Beginning at the lower edge of the taper and halfway between the front and back, a groove is cut with a 1/4-inch ball cutter .100 inch deep. This serves to allow formation of a guide rib which not only stiffens the magazine but serves to guide the cartridges as they are reduced from a double row in the magazine body to a single row at the feed lips.

It is helpful, but not absolutely necessary, to make up a 3/4-inch wide by 1/4-inch thick by 10-inch long strip of flat stock. A centerline is established and a 1/8-inch hole drilled through it at each end and as close to the ends as possible. This is placed on a matching centerline on the front side of the form block and, using the holes as drill bushings, the holes extended some 1/4 inch into the form block. Short pins cut from drill rod are cemented in these holes (in the form block) using epoxy or super glue. The glue is used because we may want them out again. These only serve to keep the sheet metal blank, which has corresponding holes drilled on its centerline, located in place during forming. Without them it may slip and ruin the part.

A form block for .45 ACP or 10mm is made in the same manner. The dimensions should be changed slightly. The width for the .45 can be .875 inch and the 10mm .800 inch. The length should also be increased to 1.300 inch.

In practice, a full-size template or pattern is drawn and transferred to the sheet metal, which is then cut to an exact size blank. The front plate of the form block is placed on the centerline of this and matching 1/8-inch holes drilled through it. It is then located in position over the pins in the form block and the front plate mounted in place. This "sandwich" is now placed in the vise with the upper side projecting slightly above the vise jaws, and blocked up on the underside so that it doesn't slip downward during forming. A fairly heavy piece of flat stock at least as long as the form block is placed along the outside of the projecting sheet metal and bumped with a heavy hammer, bending it down flat against the form block.

The sandwich is now removed from the vise, turned over, and replaced, and the projecting sheet metal side folded down as before. It is once more removed from the vise and replaced with the front side down, allowing the back to be folded over. If your sheet metal blank was laid out correctly, the edges should just meet at

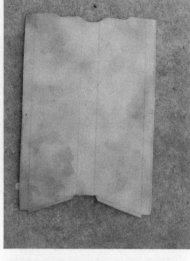

Sheet metal blank for a straight-bodied magazine.

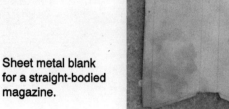

Sheet metal blank for a curved magazine.

one rear corner. If they overlap, fine. Simply trim away the edges until they just touch. If you cut it too small and there is a gap between the edges, too bad. You throw it away and start over. When it does mate satisfactorily, the seam is welded using a TIG or Heliarc process.

The upper tapered end is now bent inward, clamped, and welded down each seam at the back. Then, using a hammer and a short section of 3/16-inch flat stock with one side ground to a half round or hemispheric contour, form the cartridge guide on either side of the magazine body by swaging the ridge into the half-round cut in the form block. The lips are formed by bending the uppermost edges inward slightly and welding the rear corners. The flange on each side is bent outward 90 degrees by clamping the lower end of the magazine in the vise between two pieces of 1/2-inch flat stock with the material to be bent projecting above the surface. The flanges can be formed with a block and hammer.

The form block is removed by driving it out from the top with a rod and hammer. A semicircular cut is made at both the front and back on the top side. This will do away with the locating pin hole. The front and rear tabs are cut flush with the sides at the bottom. The bottom locating pin hole will still be there, but so what. It won't hurt anything. The welded seams can now be dressed flush. If a good welding job was done, no trace of it will remain.

Another form block should be made from flat stock. It should be just slightly wider than the flanges at the magazine bottom. This one should also have a locating pin hole through the center. Make it a 3/16-inch hole. Make a facing plate to match.

A template is made for a bottom plate that slides over the flanges at the magazine bottom, closing the bottom opening and holding the spring and follower in place. This one must be as wide as the flanges, plus a small amount for clearance and enough to fold over on top. One eighth inch wider on each side should be adequate. A hole is drilled in the center for the locating pin, the blank sandwiched between the form block and front plate, and clamped in the vise. The edges are folded using the hammer and block. A filler plate cut from the same sheet metal to fit inside the bottom plate serves as a spacer. It is placed inside the flanges and the flanges folded the rest of the way using the block and hammer. With the spacer removed, the bottom plate should just slide over the magazine flanges from the front. If it will not go on, file both the inside flanges on the plate and the outside flanges on the magazine until it does.

A matching keeper is made by cutting a strip of the sheet metal and bending the ends so that it just fits inside the magazine body. With this in place, put the bottom plate in position and mark and drill a corresponding hole through it. Silver-solder a short 3/16-inch stud in place in this hole. The magazine spring bears against this keeper, pressing it against the bottom plate with the stud engaging the hole and preventing the bottom plate from moving until the stud is pushed inward.

The follower can be made from a steel or aluminum block 1/2 inch wide, 3/4 inch deep, and 1 1/8 inch long. The top must be narrowed slightly to match the body taper. The contour of the upper side can either be rounded like the cartridge case or concave for the cartridge to lay in. The bottom side is contoured to fit inside the end of the spring.

The easiest, simplest way to come up with a magazine spring is to buy one. This, of course, is seldom possible. So round the edges on a piece of 3/8 inch wide by 1 inch flat stock about 18 inches long. Drill an .065-inch hole through one end. Take another piece of square stock 1/2 inch or 5/8 inch square and drill an .065-inch hole through it some 1/2 inch back from one end. Saw a slot that intersects the hole to a depth of 1 inch. Turn it on its side and drill and tap a hole to accept a 10 x 32 screw used to pull the slot together exerting tension on the spring wire, which passes through this hole and is fastened through the hole in the mandrel. The square bar is wound repeatedly around the mandrel using .065-inch spring wire. This is commonly known as music wire or piano wire. Made for a 30-shot magazine, such a spring should have some 24 coils spaced approximately 5/8 inch apart. Somewhere between 6 and 8 feet of wire will be required to wind this spring.

A 1/8-inch thick block 1/4 inch wide and 5/8 inch long is silver soldered in the center of the magazines backside, just below the lips. The magazine latch bears against this, holding the magazine in the gun. If you expect to make several magazines, a female die should be made up with a three-sided rectangular cross section. This can be formed by welding or bolting two lengths of 1/2 inch thick flat stock to a center section of this same material. The inside width should be .825 inch. The sides should be 1.250 inch high, measured from the inside. It should be at least 12 inches long. A slight bevel is made on the inner top walls and polished as smooth as possible. This will permit the sheet metal being formed to enter the die with as little friction as possible.

A male die is made to fit the opening in the female die, allowing twice the thickness of the material to be formed plus .003 to .005 inch for clearance. This means that if the opening in your female die measures .825 inch as recommended and you are using .036-inch thick material, you multiply .036 inch by two, which is .072 inch. Add another .003 inch for clearance, making .075 inch. When this is subtracted from .825 inch, we get .750 inch, which should be the width of the male die. This male die should be made exactly as the form block described earlier, except it should be longer to permit installation of guide pins at each end.

Place the male die inside the female die with a shim of the sheet metal on each side to keep it centered. A hole is then drilled with a 3/8-inch drill close enough to each end that room is left for the 10-inch long magazine between them. These holes are drilled through both dies while they are together. A close-fitting guide pin is inserted in each hole in the female die and silver soldered in place. The male die should slide freely on these pins.

After coating the inner lips of the female die and the outside of the sheet metal blank with a light film of grease, the blank is attached to the bottom of the male die using the locating pins and centered on top of the female die. The entire assembly is put in the vise and squeezed together, forcing the sheet metal into the die. When partway in, the vise must be backed off and a spacer block placed between the top of the male die and the vise jaw. This is to provide clearance for the protruding sheet metal, which is folded over to form the back of the magazine.

The male die and magazine body are removed from the female die, and finished as described earlier.

Magazines for most other calibers of rifle or pistol cartridges can be made in this same manner by changing the dimensions to fit. One thing that should be remembered is that double-row magazines must not be so wide that two cartridges can fit side by side. They must be somewhat narrower so that each cartridge rests somewhat on top of the one below it. Otherwise they will wad up and wedge in the magazine and fail to feed.

Due to their peculiar feeding problems, shotgun magazines must be made somewhat differently. The blunt-nosed shell will not feed dependably unless presented from the feed lips at a specific angle. Due to the fact that the rimmed base end is considerably larger in diameter than the front end, the shell noses start to dip further into the magazine as more shells are added. A straight-bodied magazine may feed with only five, sometimes six, shells in the magazine, but when more are added they start to bind at the forward end and become progressively worse as more rounds are added. To feed dependably, each shell must be presented in the same plane, regardless of how many shells are in the magazine.

The easiest way to accomplish this is to curve the magazine so that the shells will do this. The curve can be determined by placing 10 shells in the correct relationship to each other on a large piece of paper. A line is drawn along the back of the shells as well as the front. This will give you the correct curve. A line is also drawn along the length of the top shell. Enough room must be included at the bottom for the compressed spring and follower in addition to the shells. A template is made from this drawing and two identical sides cut from the sheet metal (.036 inch thick). Strips for the front and back sections are cut from thicker stock (16 gauge or .060 inch).

Since we cannot form the compound curves required to make these magazines in one piece, the four separate components must be fitted together and all four seams welded for their full length. The front and rear strips are bent to the same contour as the side panels and all four parts clamped together and welded using the TIG or Heliarc process. Care must be taken not to let the heat generated during welding spread anymore than absolutely necessary, which may cause the sides to buckle slightly. This won't affect the working but has a detrimental effect on the appearance.

Bottom flanges, bottom plate, retainer, and latch block are made in the same manner as described earlier.

The welded seams are dressed smooth and flush with the metal and the metal polished. Again, don't allow the metal to overheat while polishing. It will expand if this is allowed to happen and may buckle the sides as described above.

High-capacity (25 to 30 round) .22 rimfire magazines can be made without the usual curve if they are made wide enough, with a rib swaged lengthwise down each side of the magazine body to allow the rimmed ends to spread, or "fishtail," thereby preventing the rims from hanging up on each other. A form block is made with a groove down each side and the magazine body formed around it in the same manner already described. The rib is then swaged into each side by making up a forming tool and pressing it into the sides of the magazine using pressure from the vise. A long coil spring is used instead of the accordion type. Except for this, the magazine is made in the same manner as the others.

Chapter

Stocks

14

Making stocks for prototype firearms differs from stocking existing guns, mostly because no "preinletted semifinished" stocks are available to fit to them. While there are a few good stock makers in this country who can whittle a stock from the block, or blank, the average stock maker (perhaps fitter would be a better word), when called upon to make a stock for conventional rifles or shotguns, orders out one of the turned and inletted blanks available from numerous suppliers around the country and proceeds to fit it to the gun and finish it, maybe adding checkering if he has the skill. He then swaggers around telling anyone who will listen abut the "custom" stocks he makes. Never mind that it is almost identical to all the rest of the stocks that the particular manufacturer has turned. The only thing "custom" about it is, probably, the brand of finish used.

In our case, we are going to have to make the stock from scratch. From the block. This has never been a problem for me. I started making stocks back around the beginning of World War II, when I was 12 years old. No semifinished stocks were available due to the war effort, so I made stocks from scratch with only the information I got from Clyde Baker's gunsmithing book to guide me. Most of my stock jobs were on double-barrel side-lock shotguns. I had already made a couple hundred of these before I ever had the luxury of working with an almost finished stock when they became available again after the war.

In truth, stocking the prototype gun from scratch isn't any more difficult than stocking any other gun. We simply fit the wood to the barreled action, shape it to our taste, sand it, and apply finish.

If we are building a straight-line recoil gun, it will actually have a three-piece stock: the buttstock, grip, and forend. The buttstock and grip are held in place by through bolts. The forend surrounds the barrel and is held in place by a threaded sleeve, or nut. All three have one thing in common—they each require a lengthwise hole drilled all the way through.

Two sidelock trap guns that were restocked by the author from blocks of wood several years ago. No semifinished stocks were available for these.

The easiest way to drill these holes is to turn the stem of a drill of the size required to fit into a length of tubing. The tubing must have an outside diameter slightly smaller than the drill. If no such tubing is available, solid rod can be used by drilling a hole in one end of the same size and deep enough to accept the turned-down drill stem, which is silver soldered in place. Cool the drill quickly after silver soldering to prevent the heat used to fuse the two pieces together from spreading, as you do not want to anneal the drill.

The blank to be drilled is held between centers in the lathe, the tool post drawn up against it, and the blank clamped to the tool post. The blank can be moved to keep it centered by moving the cross slide. The tail stock center is withdrawn, the drill mounted in the lathe chuck, and the hole drilled by feeding the blank into the drill with the lathe carriage.

The large hole through the forend, and the buttstock when the telescoping spring mechanism is used, is obtained by first drilling a 3/4-inch or similar hole through it.

An adjustable drill is made up by drilling a 3/8-inch hole crosswise and on center through a piece of 3/4-inch round stock. Drill another hole to accept a 1/4 x 28-inch set screw at a right angle to and intersecting the first hole. This hole should be drilled with a .218-inch (7/32) drill and tapped 1/4 x 28 inches. A single edge cutter is ground from a discarded 3/8-inch end mill, inserted in the hole, and locked in place with the set screw. With some experimentation, this boring tool can be set to drill any size hole desired by moving the blade in or out. The diameter of the boring tool body plus twice

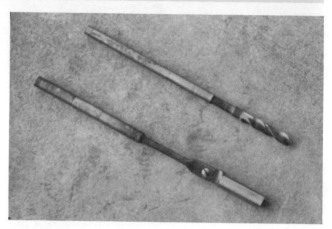

Long drills to bore stock holes.

A finished buttstock and grip mounted in place.

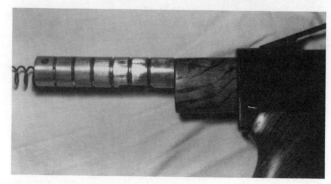

Stock piston, filler block, and spring.

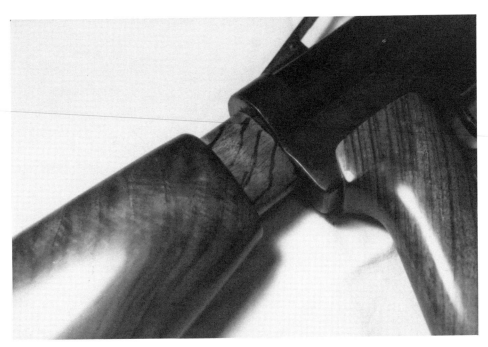

Filler block telescopes into buttstock.

the amount of blade protrusion will be the diameter of the hole drilled.

In use, the body of our boring tool is pushed through the hole in the stock blank. The drive end of the tool is held in the lathe chuck and the other end secured by the tail stock center. The blank is again clamped to the tool post and fed into the cutter with the lathe carriage.

The forend can be bored in this manner or the blank turned round first. Then it is chucked and the hole bored by first drilling a 3/4-inch hole with a drill held in the tail stock chuck, then boring to size with a boring bar held in the tool post.

The forend is then mounted on the barreled receiver and chucked in the lathe, where it is turned to the configuration desired. If a sharp, round-nosed lathe tool is used and the work turned at the highest speed possible, a fairly smooth finish will result. Rough tool marks can be removed by holding a file against the revolving work and moving it back and forth across the surface. This is followed by progressively finer grades of sandpaper, using 400 grit for the final sanding.

The buttstock and grip through bolt hole must be counterbored at the outside end to give clearance for the bolthead. This is done simply by running a drill of ample size to clear the bolthead into the hole far enough to let the mounting bolt protrude enough to screw into the receiver. After drilling with a standard angle-pointed drill, a flat-ended drill should be used to form a square, flat shoulder for the bolthead to bear against.

Whatever type of buttplate you prefer should be mounted on the butt stock before shaping and the length of pull determined. Excess wood can mostly be removed using the band saw and milling machine.

If a plastic backplate is made up from 1/8 inch thick material just slightly smaller than the flexible 7-inch sanding discs that are used mostly on disc sanders in automobile body shop and available at auto parts stores and is mounted behind the sanding disc on a 1/2 to 1 horsepower motor, the stock and grip can be shaped easily and quickly to an almost finished contour. This is followed by final shaping with wood rasps, files, and progressively finer grades of sandpaper. Needless to say, sanding should be done with the sandpaper backed up by sanding blocks. This will go a long way toward preventing high and low places or dished areas. A well-done stock should present an even, ripple-free surface when held up lengthwise and sighted along the sides. Many otherwise good stocks must be downgraded because of this.

Your favorite finish can then be applied. I have had best results, both for appearance and durability, with the oil-based finishes such as Tru-Oil, Linspeed, and the like. The instructions accompanying these finishes usually insinuate

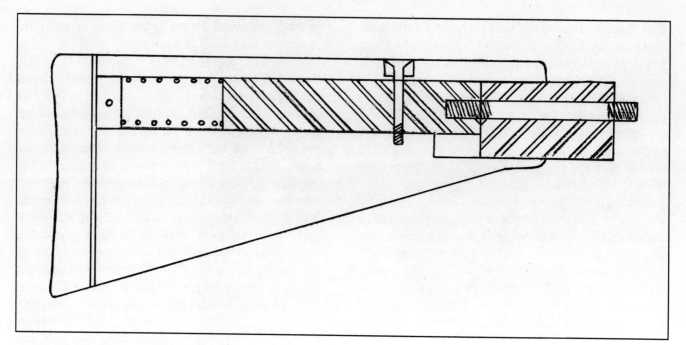

Spring-loaded, recoil-absorbing buttstock.

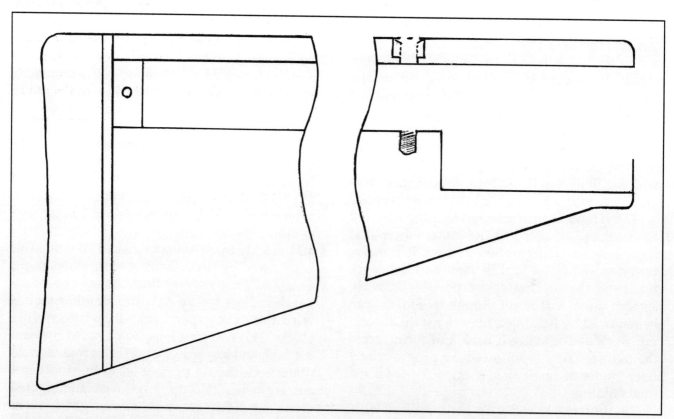

Suggested buttstock configuration. No dimensions are given since this should be shaped and sized as desired.

that three or four coats will provide a satisfactory finish. Actually, if a good, completely filled finish is anticipated, more like 15 coats will be required. The three recommended coats should be applied to the wood, allowing each to dry, of course, then sanded back to the bare wood.

There will still be unfilled pores which will show up as tiny shiny specks in the resanded wood. Repeat the process until all pores are filled. Some stock makers "whisker" their stocks before applying finish. This is done by wetting or dampening the wood, usually with a damp cloth, and allowing it to dry. This raises the grain in the form of "whiskers," which are then sanded off. Sometimes this process is repeated three or four times. In truth, when you are sanding the finish back to the wood several tines anyway, this part of the operation is mostly wasted, especially if the finish you are using is considered waterproof.

With all the pores filled, the wood is given five or six more coats of finish, allowing each to dry thoroughly. It should now be extremely smooth and free from imperfections. When you are sure the finish is completely dry, it should be rubbed down with automobile rubbing compound, followed by an application of automobile paste wax such as Turtlewax.

One-piece stocks are made in much the same manner. The stock is cut to profile using a band saw. The top side is dressed flat using the milling machine and centerlines established on both top and bottom. Holes for the stock bolts are drilled on the centerline the exact distance apart. Guide pins long enough to reach all the way through the stock are threaded and screwed into the receiver. These pins are then inserted into their corresponding holes in the stock blank and the metal parts pushed firmly against the wood. You can then mark around the outline of the receiver/barrel assembly on top and the magazine/trigger guard assembly on the bottom. Most of the excess wood can be removed with the milling machine, using ball cutters to cut the barrel channel and standard end mills for the remainder. These cuts should be slightly undersize, with the final inletting done by hand using chisels, scrapers, and rasps.

Spread a thin coating of some sort of nondrying coloring compound such as lampblack, prussian blue, or lipstick on the metal parts, then press them firmly into the stock (with the guide

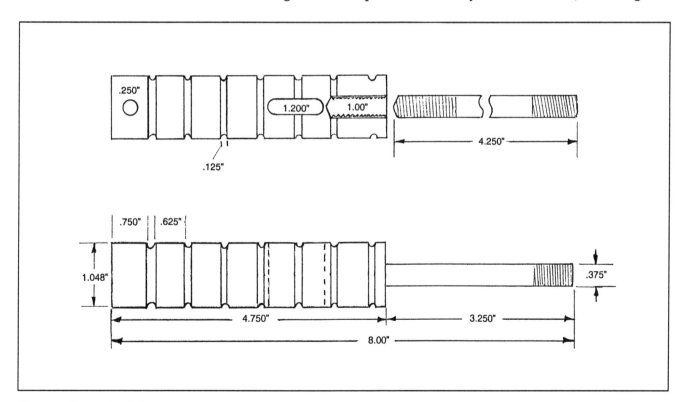

Piston and mounting bolt.

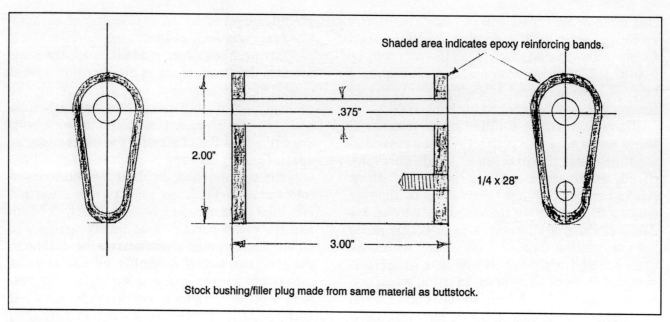

Shaded area indicates epoxy reinforcing bands.

.375"

2.00"

3.00"

1/4 x 28"

Stock bushing/filler plug made from same material as buttstock.

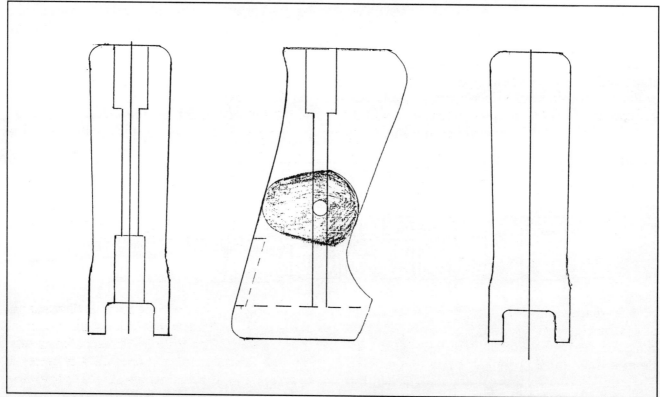

Suggested grip configuration, to be shaped and sized according to maker's requirements.

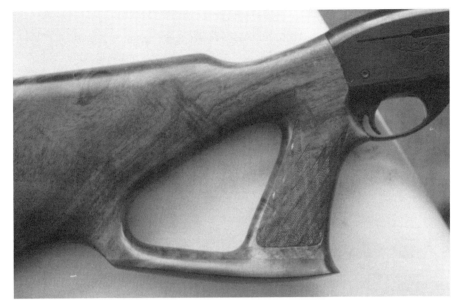

Pistol grip stock as used on a
Remington 1100.

The milling machine will cut accurate
flat surfaces.

pins in place). This will clearly mark any high spots or tight places where wood must be removed. Cut away the marked places, just a little at a time, until the metal parts fit properly. The outside is then shaped and finished in the same manner as the two-piece stock.

The telescoping, spring-loaded buttstock mentioned before will do more to tame recoil than all the recoil-reducing gadgets on the market combined. While it is better suited to two-piece stocks, it can be adapted to one-piece stocks by machining, or carving, the filler stub just behind the receiver and bolting both the grip and the stock piston to it. In almost all cases where the telescoping stock is used, the pistol-type grip is necessary.

As used in the two-piece stock, a filler stub is made up to approximately the shape shown in the drawing. One hole is drilled completely through for the stock bolt and another below it to accept a locator pin, which serves to keep the stock from turning when bolted in place.

The buttstock is drilled lengthwise to accept a liner made from aluminum tubing. The diameter of the tubing should be as close to 1 1/8 inch as possible, with an inside diameter of approximately 1 inch. A close-fitting plug, 1 inch long, is pinned in the end of the tubing that will be closest to the buttplate. It is then epoxied in place with the plugged end flush with the wood and the recoil pad both screwed and epoxied in place.

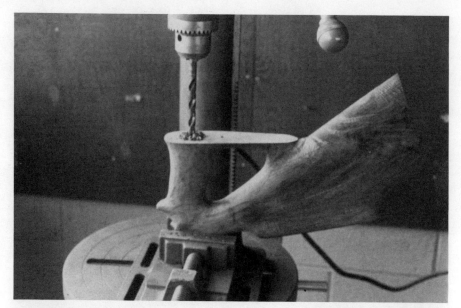

When a one-piece grip and stock are used, the grip should be reinforced. First drill a hole lengthwise through the grip.

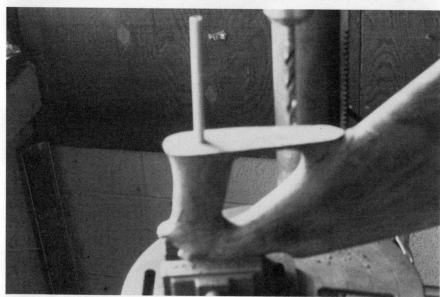

Then glue a close-fitting dowel inside it to full depth. The dowel must not protrude into the stock bolt hole.

Another hole 3/4 inch in diameter is drilled below the larger hole in the forward end of the stock. This should be 1 inch, center to center, below the top hole. This hole should be approximately 3 inches deep. It forms the lower side of the cavity cut for the filler plug to slide into. The wood left between the holes can be removed with a flat chisel. The cavity so formed should have clearance of at least 1/16 inch all the way around the filler plug.

A piston is turned from aluminum round stock to a slip-fit inside the tubing stock liner. I won't try to give an exact diameter since tubing is not always available in the exact inside diameter wanted, so we have to adapt to what is available. The tubing used in the stock pictured measures 1.049 inch inside. Therefore we made the outside diameter of the piston 1.048 inch. It is 4.750 inches long and has seven annular rings 1/8 inch wide spaced 5/8 inch apart. These rings are filled with wheel bearing grease at final assembly, which not only lubricates the sliding parts but acts in the same manner as a piston ring to give a bit of an air cushion effect, along with the spring resistance, to compression of the stock.

The forward end of the piston is drilled and tapped for the stock or mounting bolt to thread into. This bolt should be screwed in as tight as possible.

The filler plug should be reinforced against splitting or cracking by cutting a band 1/8 inch deep and 1/4 inch wide at both the front and

Boring the buttstock (above and left).

back ends completely around the circumference of the plug. The circumference of the larger outside size is wrapped with masking tape, forming a groove which is filled with epoxy. When dry, this is sanded flush with the outside surface, leaving a reinforcing band permanently attached. This filler block should then be finished completely. It is then given a heavy coat of paste wax, which, when dry, will serve as a release compound to prevent its being cemented into the stock.

The piston is also given a coating of wax or some other sort of release compound and inserted into the stock with a thick coat of silicone grease applied at the forward end of the piston to prevent any epoxy from seeping past. The inside of the stock cavity is now coated with an epoxy gel (Micro Bed works nicely) and the filler

plug slipped over the stock bolt and pushed in until it bottoms against the cavity rear wall.

When set up, this epoxy liner not only makes for a close fit between the plug and stock but also forms a reinforcing sleeve around the inside of the thin-walled stock cavity. As soon as the epoxy sets, the plug and piston should be pulled from the stock. We don't want it permanently attached, which could very well happen if it was left in place until cured completely. It should be removed, given a coat of grease, and replaced until cured completely. The entire assembly—piston, filler plug and all—should slide in and out of the stock with little or no resistance except from the air cushion effect. If it does not, the inside of the stock must be sanded until it does.

A 1/4-inch hole is drilled crosswise through the piston back close to the rear end. This is only used to insert a rod into to screw it up tight, so it doesn't matter much as to the exact location.

The piston with the filler plug in place is screwed into the receiver as tightly as possible. The stock is slipped over the piston and pushed forward to the length of pull desired with the stock in its uncompressed position. A .218-inch hole is drilled from the top side through both sides of the stock liner and the piston 3 1/2 inches to the rear of the forward lip of the stock. The stock is then removed and the top side drilled through with a .250-inch drill, which is then counterbored .250 inch deep with a .500-inch end mill to receive an aluminum or brass escutcheon. The lower side of the hole is tapped with a 1/4 x 28 inch tap.

The piston is now set up in the milling machine and, using the .218-inch hole drilled through it as a reference point, a slot .250 inch wide and 1.200 inch long is cut forward lengthwise from the existing hole. This allows the stock retaining screw to move back and forth in the slot. A .500-inch diameter escutcheon .250 inch thick and counterbored to fit the screw head is installed in the hole on the top side and a 1/4 x 28 x 1 1/2 inch screw made up to fit. The face of this screw should be radiused slightly to match the contour of the stock.

The spring used in the stock shown is .900 inch in diameter, 2.300 inches in length, and has 12 coils wound from wire measuring .092 inch in diameter.

To assemble, the piston with filler plug in place is screwed tightly into the receiver. The piston is given a thin coating of grease. The spring is then inserted in the stock hole and the stock pushed forward over it until the retaining screw can be installed and screwed in flush with the surface of the stock.

The spring, as described, has enough resistance to hold the stock in its extended position when shouldered. It also has enough elasticity to allow the stock to compress, or give, as much as 1 inch.

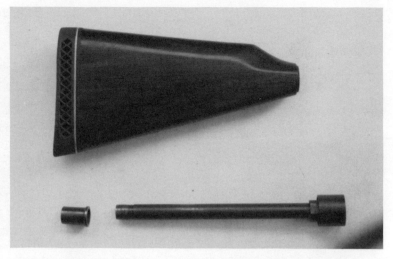
An autoloader buttstock is mounted over the action spring tube, held in place by a nut at the rear.

An adjustable buttplate is useful at times.

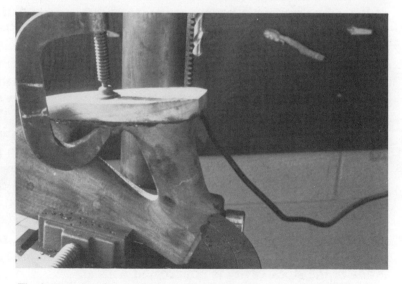
The buttstock, grip, and forend can usually be cut from one rifle blank.

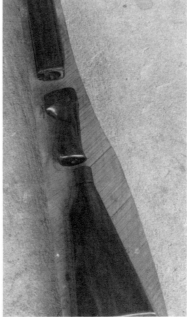

The grip cap epoxied to the stock acts as reinforcement (lleft)).

Recoil-absorbing buttstock as used on a trap gun (far left).

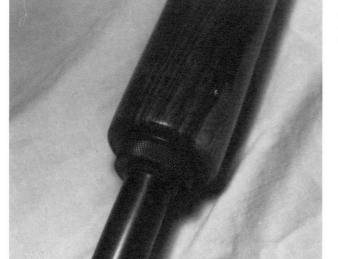

A knurled barrel nut threaded on the barrel holds the forend in place.

This will absorb quite a bit of recoil, especially in a heavy recoiling gun. A stiffer or lighter spring may be required to suit the shooter's needs.

If this stock design is used in conjunction with one of the muzzle brakes described, a comfortable shooting gun with very little recoil will result.

Chapter

Sights

15

As long as conventional designs are adhered to, sights are not a problem. We simply shop around until we find an adaptable set of commercial sights and install them on the gun. Unfortunately, when we depart from the type of firearms that are just like all the rest and try to build something different, it is often required that we build the sights too, or at least mounts to adapt off-the-shelf sights.

If building a design with a high sight line and straight-line recoil, the sight line must be around 2 inches higher than the stock comb. Whether using a telescopic, open, or aperture sight, a special mount will be required to permit this dimension. Many times this base can be used as a carrying handle. This will also necessitate a high front sight assembly to match when iron sights are used.

When made for iron-sight use, the rear base and carrying handle can be cut to shape and folded from sheet metal. The upper trough, which is formed by the bottom and two vertical sides, should have a minimum width of .625 inch. This will allow mounting commercial sights such as the Williams Guide series or the Marble Universal #20, which is a close copy of the Williams except that it is made of steel, whereas the Williams is made of aluminum. These are mounted by drilling and tapping two holes in the base and installing two screws.

A matching front sight can be made from sheet metal or machined from solid stock. Front sights of this type may require frequent removal, so some means should be incorporated to accomplish this. If the shotgun muzzle brake is used, the front sight is mounted on the upper side of it and installed and removed as a unit. When mounted directly on a barrel, some means of clamping must be used to hold it in place. While it isn't as streamlined appearance wise, the single upright machined front sight will mount securely through use of a split upper side which is tightened by a through bolt. The extended, sloping ramp type has a better appearance but requires sleeves that slip over the barrel, to be welded or silver soldered in place.

This rear sight platform is adjustable to fit the individual shooter by loosening the screw in the front upright and moving the sight portion up or down. Elevation adjustments can be made in the same manner.

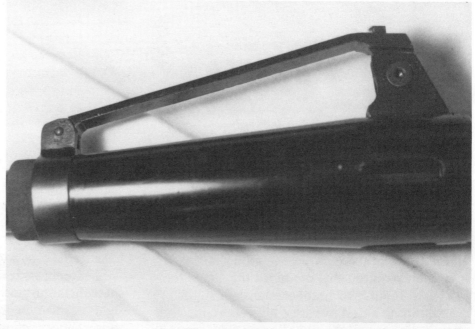

Front sight elevation adjustments are made in the same manner. Windage adjustments are made by loosening the knurled locknut at the rear of the brake body and turning the assembly in the required direction.

If an optical sight is used, the base will be somewhat shorter. It will need to be somewhat sturdier to withstand the extra weight of the scope during recoil. This cannot be folded in one piece as were the iron sight models but must be folded in three sections and welded together. If the welds are well done and dressed back flush with the surface, no visible seam will show. Special bases must be made that will hold the scope in place through use of two thumbscrews.

Shotgun ribs are made up, either as full-length ribs or two short adjustable sections. The short two-piece ribs will continue to gain in popularity as more shooters become acquainted with them. Not only are they lighter in weight and offer less wind resistance than the full-length rib, but visibility is also increased. When the rear rib is adjusted to fit the shooter exactly, the front rib is then adjusted to move the point of impact to where the shooter wants it. When this is done, the open space between the ribs will not be visible to the shooter. Stock comb height is no longer critical since the rib adjustments will permit correct drop regardless of comb height, within reason.

Steel-tube muzzle brake with adjustable front sight.

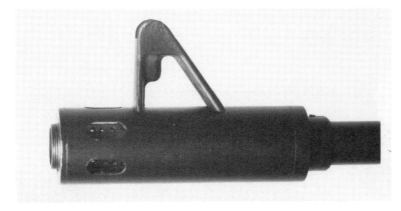

Steel-tube muzzle brake with fixed front sight.

The short ribs each consist of three separate parts. The rib body is the long sloping section. A rear base is fixed to the receiver or barrel. The rear end of the rib is hinged to this base and held in place with a crosspin, which allows the rib to move up and down. A front base, or post, is slotted to receive a tongue, which comprises the front leg of the rib. The front base is attached in place at the forward end of the receiver or, in the case of the forward rib, to the barrel or muzzle brake body. A cross screw clamps the outside sections of the front base together against the tongue of the rib through tightening the cross-mounted screw, which is also loosened to permit adjustment.

The ribs can be made from steel or aluminum. The aluminum one will be lighter in weight, but it will be harder to finish since it will require anodizing or painting. The steel rib is easily finished by any of several bluing processes.

Whichever material is used, the rib is cut from 3/8-inch flat stock. The front leg is cut to a thickness of 1/8 inch by machining

Rear sight made of folded sheet metal and silver soldered in place, as used on assault-type pistols.

Front sight to match the rear sight in previous photo.

metal from each side, as is a short section at the rear that fits into a slot in the rear base. The ribs can be profiled by sawing and machined to finished shape with the milling machine. The steel ribs can be made as a straight section and the slope formed by bending. The slope in the aluminum rib should be machined to shape, since the aluminum may very well crack or break if you attempt to bend it. A flat-bottomed groove should be cut lengthwise along the top section of the rear rib with a 1/8-inch end mill. This is simply a sighting aid since the groove attracts the shooter's eye to the center of the rib. The front rib is drilled and tapped at the forward end for whatever type of front sight the shooter desires.

The rear base and front post are also cut from 3/8-inch flat, stock. Those to be mounted on the receiver must be made of steel since they will be welded or silver soldered in place. A front post that will be attached to the muzzle brake with screws can be made from aluminum if desired. These parts are cut to shape and contoured on the bottom to closely fit the surface they are attached to. The front posts must have a longitudinal slot cut almost to the bottom of the post, which fits the rib tongue closely. Likewise, the rear mount must be slotted to accept the narrow tongue section at the rear of the rib. The upper front edge of the rib base is radiused and a matching concave cut made at the rear upper edge of the rib. This allows the hinged movement without an unsightly gap.

"Express" type rear sight with folding leaves dovetailed into the quarter rib.

Banded ramp sight to match the rear sight in previous photo.

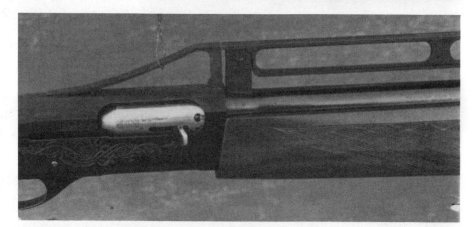

Adjustable-impact high rib on a Remington 1100.

High rib with adjustable point of impact on one of my own guns. This one is adjustable at both front and rear.

Truss-type ribs are machined from solid stock.

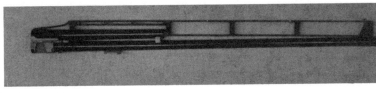

Truss-type rib used in "unsingle" conversion.

A knurled collar locks the front sight assembly in place. When loosened, windage adjustments can be made.

Vertical point-of-impact changes are made by loosening the screw and shifting the rib up or down as desired.

When fitted together in their assembled relationship, the rear base is drilled for a 1/8-inch crosspin, as is the rib projection. Drill the hole first with a No. 31 drill followed by a 1/8-inch drill. Go through only one side of the base and the rib projection with the larger drill. The slightly smaller hole in the opposite side will exert enough friction on the pin to keep it in place.

The front post is drilled, with the rib in place, and tapped for a 10 x 32 screw. This should be a countersunk-head Allen screw. The screw hole is countersunk so that the screw head is flush with the surface of the post when the screw is tight. The hole through the rib tongue is lengthened to form a slot which will allow the rib to move up and down with the loosened screw in place.

If mounted on the barrel, the rear base for the front rib is made in the same way described above. If used on the muzzle-brake equipped gun, the base is joined to a round ring which fits

over the rear end of the muzzle brake. This permits adjustment for windage, since the lock nut at the rear of the muzzle brake can be loosened and the muzzle brake and rib assembly rotated to shift the pattern horizontally.

Any number of people will tell you (and firmly believe) that the sights on a shotgun don't make any difference since they don't see them anyway. Such was the case with an acquaintance of mine, who is also one of the better trap shooters in this area. He brought by my shop a Kreighoff combination set that he had traded for and asked me to look it over and see if I thought it needed anything.

This guy is such a complete cheapskate that he will make his family go to bed before dark so that he doesn't have to pay for electricity to light his house, so I didn't really have a lot of enthusiasm for even looking at his gun. It was obvious, however, that some amateur gunsmith had installed a middle sight that was nowhere close to the middle of the rib. It also leaned at about a 10-degree angle. When I pointed this out to him, he said he already knew it but he would leave it that way since he never saw the sights when he shot. That was fine with me. It was none of my business anyway, so I handed him back his gun and told him it looked good to me.

A few days later he brought it back. He said he needed the middle sight straightened up and put in the middle of the rib. He said that he had been to a trapshoot over the preceding weekend and couldn't hit anything with the gun. One of the self-appointed coaches who are always on hand around a gun club had watched him shoot and told him he was canting the gun. At this point, he said, he realized that he was unconsciously trying to align the middle sight, which caused him to cant the gun. I started once to tell him to do the work himself, since he was so smart, but I didn't. I removed the off-center sight, plugged the hole, and installed another the way it was supposed to be. After that he could hit with the gun. He now understands that he does see his sights, even though he isn't aware of it. So does almost everyone else. Therefore, we will go ahead and install the sights in a way that will permit a person who admits to using the sights to hit with the gun. This will allow the one who don't see the sights to do likewise.

Full-length truss-type ribs can be machined from flat stock. Checkering, knurling, curved lines, or whatever other type of finishing is desired is cut or rolled into the upper side of the rib. This is both for ornamentation and to render the surface less light reflective. This should be done first, since the solid material is easier held on edge and far stiffer than when machined to shape.

A checkered pattern can be rolled into the

Fixed sights are used on both these guns, with no adjustment possible. This arrangement is adequate for nontarget guns.

upper side by making up a round shanked holder to contain a knurling head. With the rib material mounted securely to the milling machine table, either with two or more vises or by clamps, the knurling tool is mounted in the quill and aligned with the work. With down pressure on the knurling tool, the rib blank is drawn lengthwise under it, either with the handwheel or using the power feed. This will roll a knurled checkering pattern into the face of the rib. Needless to say, the knurling tool must be held in line with the rib. If the quill cannot be locked and prevented from rotating on your milling machine, a guide should be made and clamped to the side of the tool to keep it from turning. This design looks even better with a 1/8-inch flat, shallow groove cut down the center of the rib using a 1/8-inch end mill, before the knurling is done.

If the milling machine is equipped with a power feed, slightly curved crosswise grooves, or crosshatching, equally spaced along the top of the rib can be cut through use of a fly cutter or face mill. A single cutting tool is used, and the head must be angled enough that the cutter only contacts the rib surface on one side during each

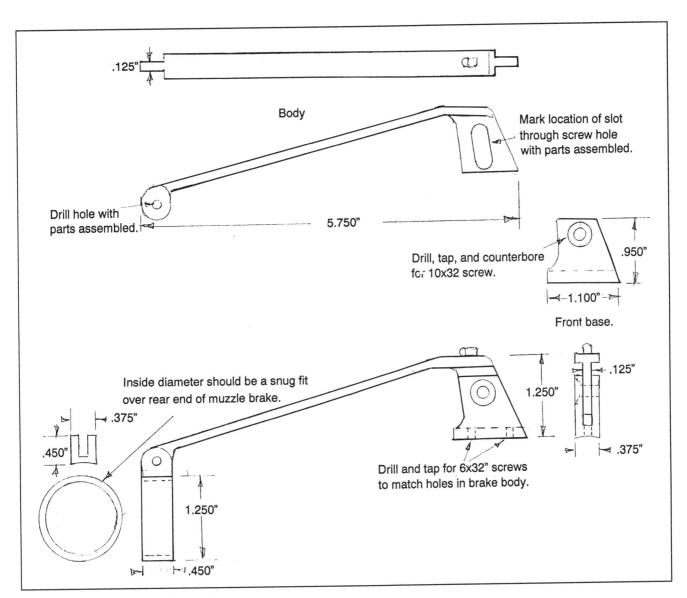

.125"

Body

Mark location of slot through screw hole with parts assembled.

Drill hole with parts assembled.

5.750"

Drill, tap, and counterbore for 10x32 screw.

.950"

1.100"

Front base.

Inside diameter should be a snug fit over rear end of muzzle brake.

.375"

.450"

1.250"

1.250"

.125"

.375"

Drill and tap for 6x32" screws to match holes in brake body.

.450"

Adjustable front sight assembly for shotgun use.

revolution of the tool. Only a shallow cut is required to form sharp-topped grooves. So the tool depth should be set at .015 to .025 inch and the machine started with the cutter not quite contacting the end of the rib. The power feed is now engaged, which moves the material under the cutter and cuts a new groove with each revolution of the cutter. The number of lines per inch and the shape of the grooves can be varied by using different diameter tool holders and varying the speed of the power feed. It would be wise to experiment on scrap material before attempting the actual job. Changing the quill speed will also cause variations in the pattern.

Light weight of the finished rib is desirable, so all excess material possible should be removed.

Except for coloring problems, aluminum is probably the best material to use for this. A full-width rib is left at the top, plus a short section at the front and rear which will enclose a fixed rib post and allow vertical adjustment. The bottom should also retain a full-width section. Several vertical posts, or spaces, should be laid out of equal width and an equal distance apart between the front and rear ends. All excess material is now cut from between the spacers. The spacers themselves, as well as a narrow ridge along the top and bottom, are cut to a thickness of 1/8 inch. These ridges contribute to the overall stiffness while contributing to reduced weight and thus should not be neglected.

The full thickness section at the front of the

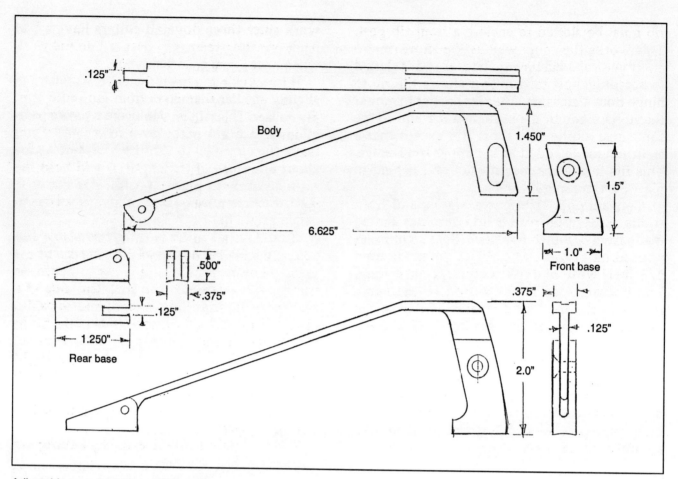

Adjustable rear sight assembly for shotgun use.

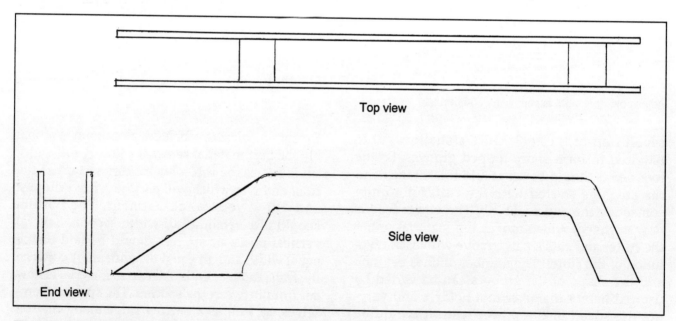

The rear sight base/carrying handle is folded from 14-gauge sheet metal. It can be made in three pieces and welded at bends or made in one piece, sawed-through vertical uprights bent to contour, and fillets welded into the open spaces. Overall shape or contour is to individual taste.

rib must be slotted to enclose a front rib post. This works the same way as the short ribs to effect vertical adjustment. The rear end is slotted to accept a short tongue that allows the rib to hinge from a crosspin. The rear hanger to mount the rib is made in the same manner and to the same size as the rear short rib, except that a short tongue is added at the upper front hinge. This fits inside the rear rib slot and is held in place by a crosspin.

Conventional sight bases, sights, and front sights as used on pistols and carbines can be made from 3/8-inch flat stock. Rear sight bases as used on pistols and carbines are made from 5/8 inch wide material cut 1 1/8 inch long. The bottom side is contoured to the same radius as the receiver diameter. The ends can be squared, rounded, or scalloped as desired. A crosswise dovetail is cut .100 inch deep using a standard 3/8 inch x 60 degree dovetail cutter. This slot should first be cut to full depth with a 1/4-inch end mill and finished with the dovetail cutter. This not only saves wear on the more expensive cutter but is also something of a safety precaution to prevent ruining the

work since these dovetail cutters have a bad habit of eating their way deeper into the work when heavy cuts are attempted.

It is possible to obtain the dovetail cutters in slightly smaller diameters from gunsmith supply houses. This will let you make separate passes down each side of the dovetail cut, and if you leave the slot .005 to .010 inch undersize for about one third of its length, it will hold the sight securely in place. If a full-size cutter is used, the sight must be made slightly oversize to obtain a tight fit.

If no dovetail cutter is readily available and you only intend to do one job, the slot can be cut to shape by hand. The slot is cut to depth, as before, with a 1/4-inch end mill. One side of a triangular file is ground smooth and the sides filed to shape using the smooth side of the file in the bottom of the slot and the angled sides doing the cutting. Using a file such as this, a slight taper can be cut in the length of the slot, even the ones cut with the dovetail cutter. This will cause the sight to fit progressively tighter as it is pushed in place.

The rear sight blade is made by cutting the

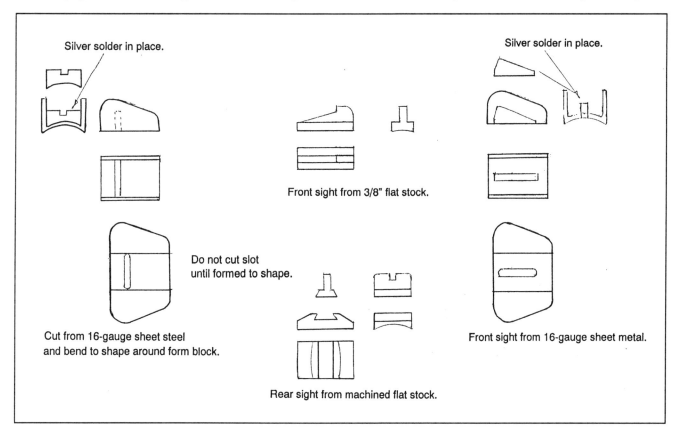

Fixed sights for use on assault-type pistols. Dimensions to suit applications.

material to an inverted T crossection. The thin leg should be .100 inch thick, with a .125 inch section at the bottom left a full .375 inch wide. It must be at least as wide as the base, and tall enough to be compatible with the front sight. If you turn it upside down and clamp it in the milling machine vise, the same dovetail cutter used to cut the base slot can be used to cut a matching angle down each side to fit into the dovetail. When you are satisfied with the length and width of the sight blade, a square notch should be cut. It is centered exactly between the outer edges and as deep as it is wide. While a matter of preference, the notch will usually be cut with a 1/8-inch end mill. The front side can be thinned with a concave relief cut using a 1/2-inch end mill.

Front sights are made in similar fashion, also using the inverted T configuration. The upright blade should be .100 to .125 inch thick and of sufficient height and width to allow shaping to the desired contour. This one, too, is turned upside down and held in the mill vise. Using a ball cutter, the bottom side is contoured to match the surface it is to be mounted on.

The base and front sight described will usually be mounted by silver soldering them in place. Extreme care should be taken to assure that both are located on the exact top centerline. This applies equally to the other bases and carrying handles as well as the ribs.

Quarter ribs are made from 1/2-inch square stock. Key stock is ideal for this purpose. The bottom side must be cut to fit the contour of the barrel. This isn't easy to accomplish, since several diameters and tapers are involved. Probably the easiest way is to cut a concave section to fit the cylindrical portion at the extreme rear. Cut the sharper tapered portion to match the barrel contour as closely as possible and the long tapered portion just ahead of it. It is cut slightly deeper than required, using a slightly smaller ball cutter than would normally be used. This will leave a thin outer edge. The blank is then clamped in place on the barrel and hit a few good licks with a hammer. The bottom contour will then conform to the barrel. It can be mounted using screws and low-temperature solder. Whatever dovetails are required to mount sights are cut after the rib is mounted on the barrel.

Front sights are made from flat stock, with the bottom contoured to match the barrel and shaped as desired. The sight blade can be machined as an integral part or a dovetail cut for insert-type sights. If a front ramp with a barrel band is required, a hole slightly smaller than the barrel diameter is bored lengthwise through a big enough block of steel to make the sight. All excess material is then cut away, leaving a short length to encircle the barrel, and the ramp formed as before.

When designing and making sights, always keep in mind that the projectile, whether it be bullet or shot charge, begins to drop the instant it leaves the barrel. Therefore the rear sight must be somewhat higher in relation to the bore than the front sight. This is necessary because the bore line must be elevated at a shallow angle to the sight line in order for the projectile to cross and pass above the sight line a short distance from the muzzle and travel in an arc until it once again crosses the sight line as it moves downward. This is the point where it will strike the target at the aiming point.

It is recommended that when using fixed sights, the rear sight should be left somewhat taller than required. This will allow it to be cut to the required height after the gun is fired and the point of impact determined. While this is a trial and error method, it is still the easiest way to establish correct sight height.

Chapter

Building a Gun

16

Using what we have discussed and learned in the previous chapters, it is time to put it into practice and actually build a gun. The example used herein is a 12-gauge slide-action military and police gun with a 10-shot detachable box magazine. Other types and calibers can be fabricated using similar methods.

As recommended earlier, we will build the magazine first. Since it is not practical to form the compound curves required in the small shop, we will have to weld up the magazine body using four sheet metal components. Cut the two sides to shape, making sure they are identical, and the two end plates. These are bent to match the curves in the side panels. With the four parts clamped in their respective positions, the four seams must be welded for their entire length and then ground flat and smooth. This is a hard way to get a magazine, but at least it is a way. The bottom plate is cut to shape from the same 20-gauge sheet metal and the sides folded to correspond with the flanges bent outward at the lower end of the magazine body. The follower is bent to shape as shown. Likewise the bottom cap retainer. The magazine feed lips are bent inward and welded to the backplate. A small block is silver-soldered in place on the backplate for the magazine latch to engage and hold the magazine in place in the gun. The spring should be wound or bent to shape from .065-inch spring wire, commonly known as piano wire or music wire.

The upper receiver is cut to length from 1 1/2 inch outside diameter 4130 seamless tubing with a .120 inch wall thickness. The front end is threaded to accommodate the barrel retainer nut and the various openings cut to the dimensions given. The blocks for the front and rear mounting bolts are welded in place on the lower side. A guide must be fastened inside the receiver to hold the bolthead in its open position during its fore and aft travel. Three 1/8-inch slots are milled in the upper receiver as shown and matching tabs milled on the guide. These are mated together and welded in place.

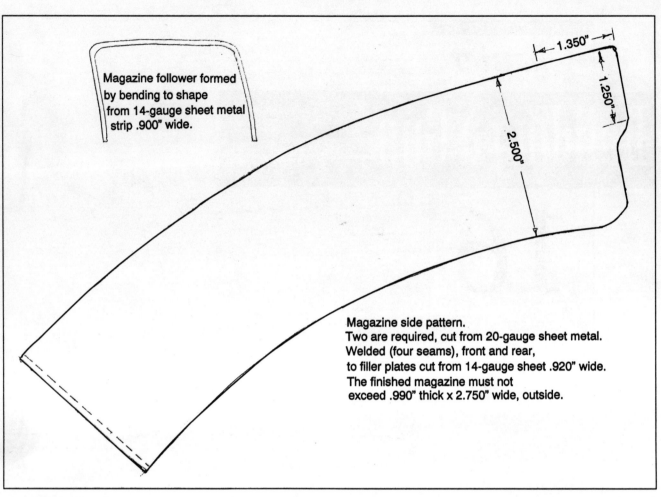

Magazine follower formed
by bending to shape
from 14-gauge sheet metal
strip .900" wide.

1.350"

1.250"

2.500"

Magazine side pattern.
Two are required, cut from 20-gauge sheet metal.
Welded (four seams), front and rear,
to filler plates cut from 14-gauge sheet .920" wide.
The finished magazine must not
exceed .990" thick x 2.750" wide, outside.

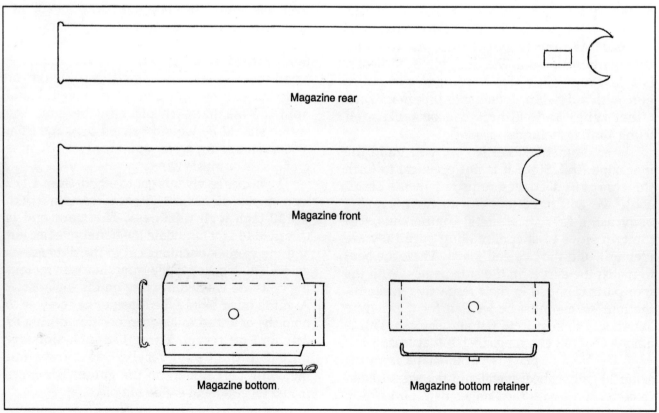

Magazine rear

Magazine front

Magazine bottom

Magazine bottom retainer

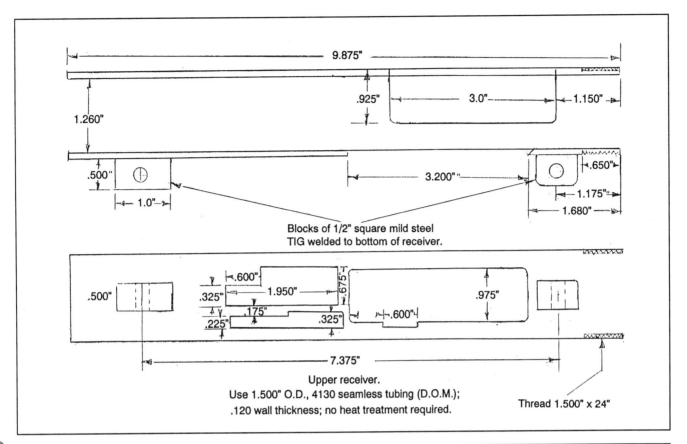

9.875"

.925"

3.0"

1.150"

1.260"

.500"

1.0"

.650"

3.200"

1.175"

1.680"

Blocks of 1/2" square mild steel
TIG welded to bottom of receiver.

.500"

.600"

1.950"

.675"

.975"

.325"

.175"

.325"

.600"

.225"

7.375"

Upper receiver.
Use 1.500" O.D., 4130 seamless tubing (D.O.M.);
.120 wall thickness; no heat treatment required.

Thread 1.500" x 24"

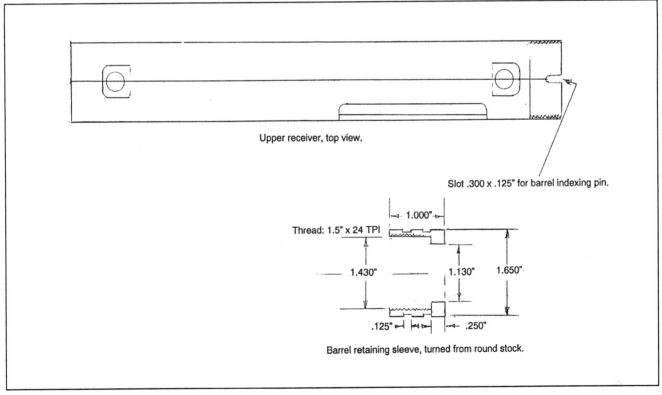

Upper receiver, top view.

Slot .300 x .125" for barrel indexing pin.

Thread: 1.5" x 24 TPI

1.000"

1.430"

1.130"

1.650"

.125"

.250"

Barrel retaining sleeve, turned from round stock.

A barrel is turned to the dimensions given. The overall length can be increased if desired, but keep in mind that the legal minimum length is 18 inches, measured from the face of the closed bolt to the muzzle, not including screw-detachable muzzle attachments. Make sure yours is at least that.

Turn the barrel extension to an outside diameter that is a slip fit inside the receiver tube, leaving a flange at the end just smaller than the root diameter of the barrel thread. The forward end is threaded to mate with the barrel thread. The rear end is tapered, forming a shallow approach cone. The counterbore for the bolt lugs is cut with a boring bar ground to form square edges. With the barrel extension in place in the receiver, scribe around the outline of the ejection port. The material within the outline is removed with the milling machine. A slot slightly wider and deeper than required is cut in the right side to clear the action bar. The bolt lug slots can be cut with a 1/2-inch end mill but should not be finished until the bolt is made.

The bolt body is turned to size and length and bored for the firing pin and bolthead. The function of the angled slot at the top is to cam the bolthead into and out of its locked position. The flat cut at the upper front is simply to provide clearance for the barrel extension. The narrow slots on the lower side provide clearance for the ejector, disconnector, and bolt lock. The wide slot on the right side with the notch at the end mates with the action bar, securing it in place. The lengthwise slot at the top provides clearance for a guide rail, which holds the bolt-head in the open position during its longitudinal travel. If not for this, it would try to rotate closed just as soon as it met resistance from the shell in the magazine.

The bolthead is turned to size leaving an oversize flange at the front that will be cut away partially to form the bolt lugs. The firing pin hole is drilled from the front end into the bolt face with a No. 31 drill at least 1 inch deep. It is then reversed in the chuck and drilled with a No. 29 drill to a 2 inch depth. The larger diameter is only to provide clearance for most of the length of the firing pin body, thereby reducing friction.

Note that the four locking lugs are not spaced evenly around the circumference of the bolt. This is necessary to provide clearance for the ejector and the ejection port. The bolt lugs are formed by removing all excess material possible with the milling machine and finishing with files and abrasive cloth. A high-speed hand grinder is useful here. The extractor cuts can be made, as can the extractor spring pockets, and the hinge pin holes drilled. Do not drill the hole for the rotating pin yet.

The bolthead lugs and slots in the barrel extension are now finished to a point where the

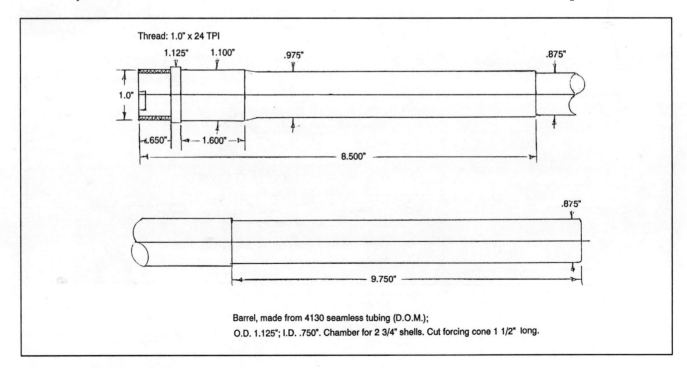

Thread: 1.0" x 24 TPI

1.125"   1.100"   .975"   .875"

1.0"

.650"   1.600"

8.500"

.875"

9.750"

Barrel, made from 4130 seamless tubing (D.O.M.);
O.D. 1.125"; I.D. .750". Chamber for 2 3/4" shells. Cut forcing cone 1 1/2" long.

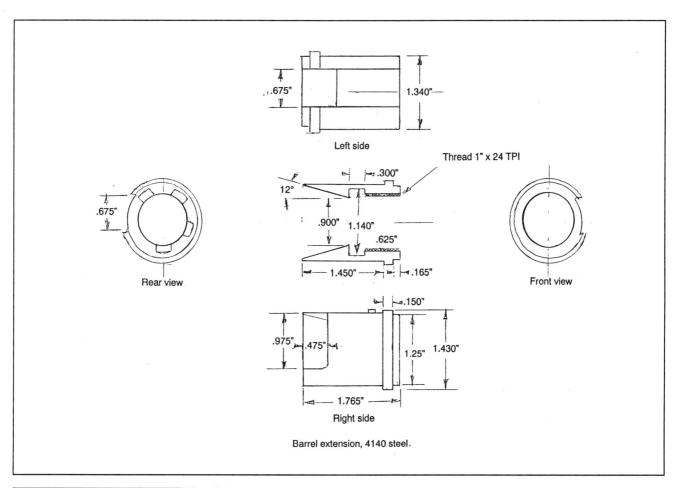

Left side

Thread 1" x 24 TPI

12°

Rear view

Front view

Right side

Barrel extension, 4140 steel.

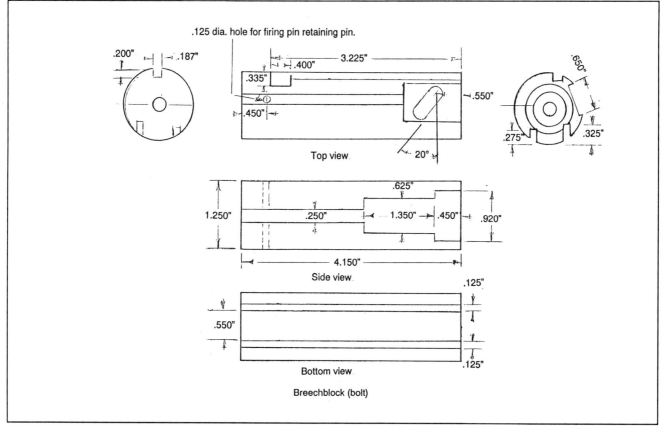

.125 dia. hole for firing pin retaining pin.

Top view

20°

Side view

Bottom view

Breechblock (bolt)

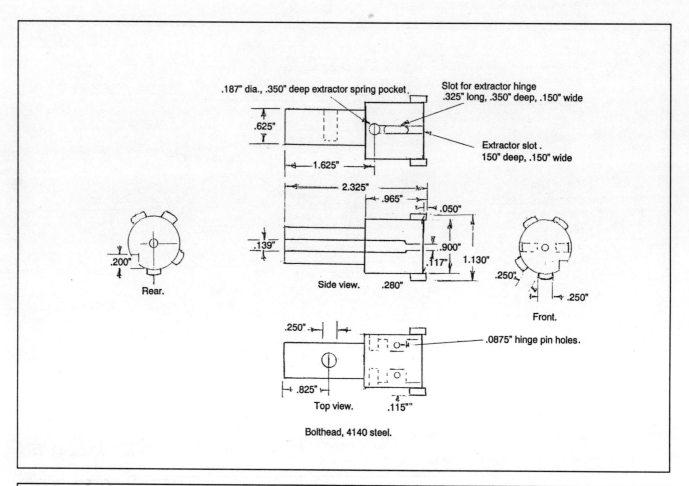

.187" dia., .350" deep extractor spring pocket.

Slot for extractor hinge
.325" long, .350" deep, .150" wide

.625"

1.625"

Extractor slot .
150" deep, .150" wide

2.325"

.965"

.050"

.139"

.900"

.117"

1.130"

.200"

Rear.

Side view.

.280"

.250"

.250"

Front.

.250"

.0875" hinge pin holes.

.825"

Top view.

.115"

Bolthead, 4140 steel.

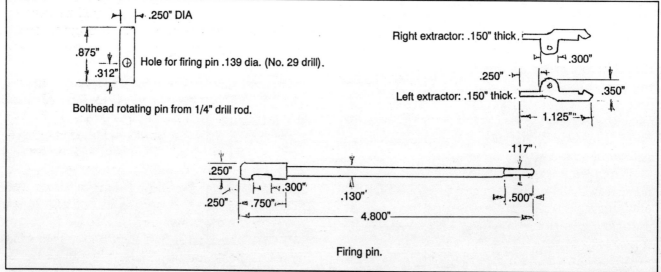

.250" DIA

.875"

.312"

Hole for firing pin .139 dia. (No. 29 drill).

Bolthead rotating pin from 1/4" drill rod.

Right extractor: .150" thick.

.300"

.250"

Left extractor: .150" thick.

.350"

1.125"

.117"

.250"

.300"

.130"

.500"

.250"

.750"

4.800"

Firing pin.

locking lugs will enter the slots and rotate into the locked position. The bolt body is pushed into its forwardmost position and the hole for the rotating pin marked and drilled. With the rotating pin in place, the No. 29 drill is used in the firing pin hole to drill through it so that the firing pin fits through the rotating pin when

assembled. The firing pin is turned to the size and shape shown and notched for the retaining pin, which fits crosswise through the bolt body.

The two extractors are made from .156-inch flat stock, placed in position in the bolthead, and the hinge pin holes drilled. Two short lengths of small coil spring that will fit into the spring

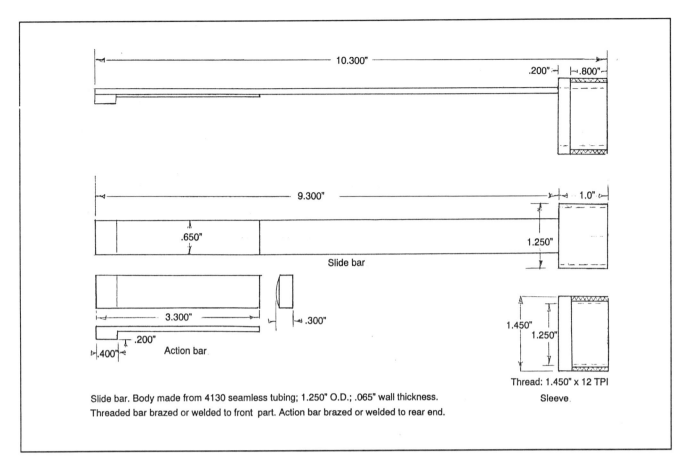

Slide bar. Body made from 4130 seamless tubing; 1.250" O.D.; .065" wall thickness.
Threaded bar brazed or welded to front part. Action bar brazed or welded to rear end.

Slide bar

Action bar

Thread: 1.450" x 12 TPI
Sleeve

pockets are inserted and the extractors pinned in place. The extractors must spring open enough for a casehead to pass between them. Paint the extreme forward ends of the extractors with a thin coat of lipstick and push the bolt as far into the barrel extension as it will go. The lipstick will mark the barrel end where the relief cuts to clear the extractors will start. These relief cuts must allow the bolthead to rotate to the locked position with a shell in the chamber.

When correctly done, as the bolt body is pushed to the rear, the cam slot turns the rotating pin, causing the bolthead to likewise turn into the unlocked position, whereby the bolt is free to travel to the rear. When the bolt is pulled forward, it rotates the bolthead in the opposite direction into its locked position. The cam surfaces and locking surfaces must be very smooth and free from burrs and tool marks. A worthwhile finishing touch is to coat the mating surfaces with a very fine-grit paste lapping compound and work them together until smooth.

A 1/8 inch wide slot is cut through the top of the threaded end of the receiver. This begins at the forward edge and extends to the rear 1/4

inch. Slide the barrel assembly into the receiver and turn it to the exact position it will be in when finished. Using the slot just cut as a guide, drill a hole 1/8 inch deep into the barrel extension using a No. 31 drill. Taper the end of a short piece of 1/8-inch drill rod slightly and drive it into this hole. It must then be ground off until it only projects about .080 inch above the surface of the barrel extension. This pin serves to locate the barrel consistently during takedown and assembly.

The action bar should be made from 1/4-inch outside diameter seamless tubing with an .065 inch wall thickness. A section at one end is left in the solid diameter and the remainder cut away, leaving a strip 5/8 inch wide. This strip serves as the action bar. A short length of 1 1/2-inch tubing with a .120 wall thickness is threaded, cut to length, slipped over the full diameter portion of the action bar, and silver-soldered in place. The action bar lug is attached to the other end in the same manner.

Make the forend by boring a hole lengthwise through a piece of 2 inch diameter black nylon that is cut to the desired length and the ends squared. The hole should be slightly larger than

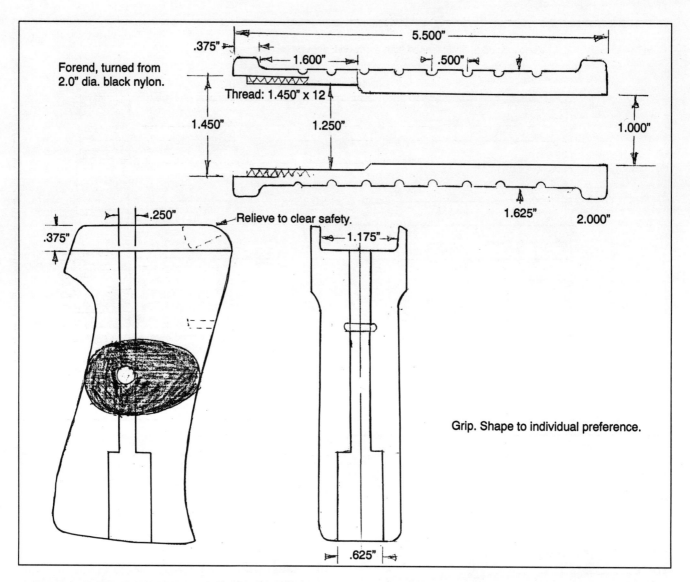

Forend, turned from 2.0" dia. black nylon.

Thread: 1.450" x 12

.375"

1.600"

.500"

5.500"

1.450"

1.250"

1.000"

1.625"

2.000"

.375"

.250"

Relieve to clear safety.

1.175"

Grip. Shape to individual preference.

.625"

the barrel diameter. One end is bored and threaded to screw onto the action bar. The outside is turned to the shape shown, or whatever contour suits you.

A barrel-retaining nut is made and threaded to screw onto the receiver, bearing against the flange at the front of the barrel extension and holding the barrel in place. The outside diameter should be knurled. Both for appearance and to facilitate tightening and loosening by hand. Knurled surfaces can be enhanced appearance wise by leaving narrow bands along the surface with slight grooves between them and knurling the bands. Using this method, the knurling tool is fed straight in, without sideways movement, on each raised band. This results in sharp, well-defined, even diamonds that may be hard to obtain in a continuous lengthwise knurl.

If the muzzle brake is used, a front sight can be made by cutting an M16 front sight shorter and silver soldering it to the body, or an adjustable front sight can be made as shown in Chapter 15.

If everything is the way it should be, you should be able to put the upper receiver/barrel assembly together now. Screw the forend on the action bar, put the barrel nut over the action bar, and insert the barrel inside. The bolt is added in place and the assembly inserted into the receiver. The barrel nut is screwed onto the receiver, forming a solid assembly.

The rear sight/carrying handle assembly is cut from 14-gauge sheet metal and bent to shape around a form block. The lower legs are bent to shape and a 1/4-inch hole drilled through each of the mounting tabs. It is now located in place

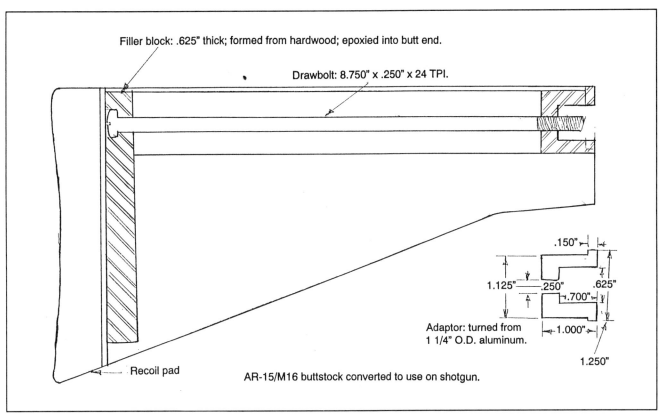

Filler block: .625" thick; formed from hardwood; epoxied into butt end.

Drawbolt: 8.750" x .250" x 24 TPI.

.150"

1.125" .250" .625"

.700"

Adaptor: turned from
1 1/4" O.D. aluminum.

1.000"

1.250"

Recoil pad

AR-15/M16 buttstock converted to use on shotgun.

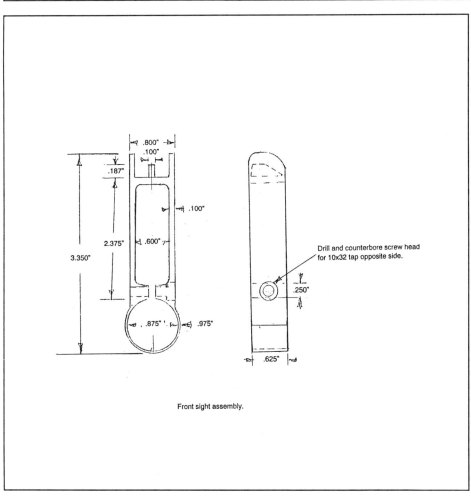

.800"

.100"

.187"

.100"

2.375" .600"

3.350"

.875" .975"

Drill and counterbore screw head
for 10x32 tap opposite side.

.250"

.625"

Front sight assembly.

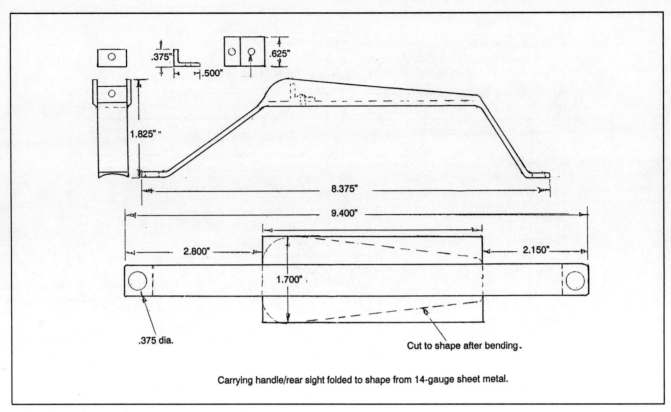

.375"
.500"
.625"

1.825"

8.375"

9.400"

2.800"

1.700"

2.150"

.375 dia.

Cut to shape after bending.

Carrying handle/rear sight folded to shape from 14-gauge sheet metal.

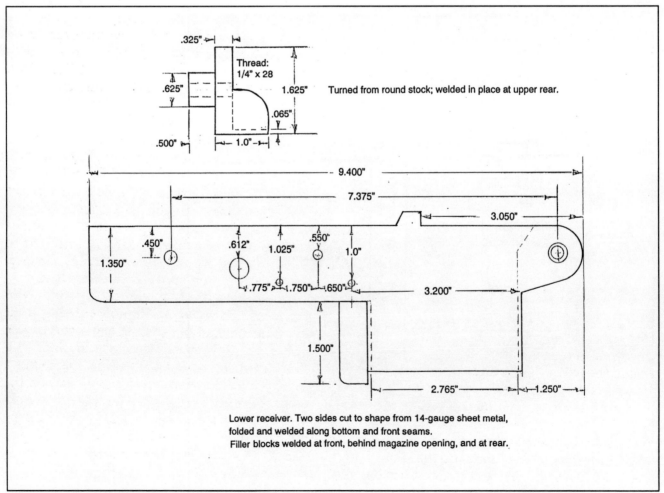

.325"

Thread:
1/4" x 28

.625"

1.625"

.065"

.500"

1.0"

Turned from round stock; welded in place at upper rear.

9.400"

7.375"

3.050"

.450"

.612"

1.025"

.550"

1.0"

1.350"

.775"

.750"

.650"

3.200"

1.500"

2.765"

1.250"

Lower receiver. Two sides cut to shape from 14-gauge sheet metal,
folded and welded along bottom and front seams.
Filler blocks welded at front, behind magazine opening, and at rear.

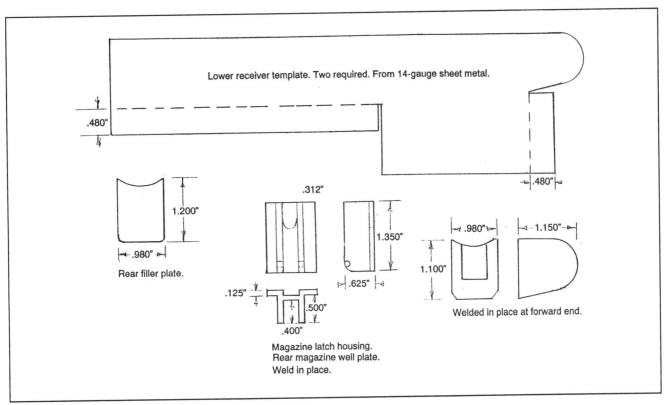

Lower receiver template. Two required. From 14-gauge sheet metal.

.480"

.480"

1.200"

.980"

Rear filler plate.

.312"

1.350"

.625"

.125"

.500"

.400"

Magazine latch housing.
Rear magazine well plate.
Weld in place.

.980"

1.150"

1.100"

Welded in place at forward end.

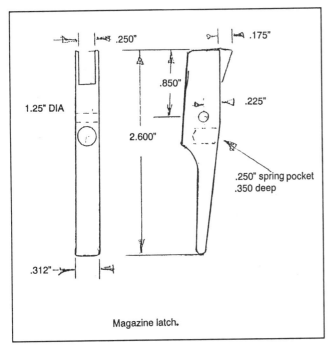

.250"

.175"

.850"

1.25" DIA

.225"

2.600"

.250" spring pocket
.350 deep

.312"

Magazine latch.

and welded to the receiver by putting the weld inside the holes. When dressed smooth, no evidence of the welding will show.

Using the pattern shown, cut two lower receiver sides and bend the bottom flanges to the inside. If possible these should be clamped to a 1 inch thick spacer block and the seam along the bottom welded. The respective filler blocks are then welded in place and the seams ground smooth. The upper side that mates against the upper receiver is milled flat and radiused inside using a 1 1/2-inch ball cutter to a close fit with the round-bodied receiver. The front filler block is cut out to mate with the front mounting bracket on the upper receiver. When fitted satisfactorily, both receivers are clamped together and the hole for the crossbolt drilled, threaded, and counterbored for the screw head. The grip mounting bolt hole is located by holding the grip in place and marking the hole through the bolt hole in the grip. This hole extends through the bottom of the lower receiver and through the rear mounting bracket, which is threaded to accommodate the grip bolt that holds the grip, lower receiver, and upper receiver together.

The buttstock is adapted from a surplus M16 stock by turning an aluminum bushing to fit into the front end of the stock and a similar one at the rear. This assembly is held in place by a long drawbolt, made by threading one end of a section of drill rod and welding a head on the other. A screwdriver slot can be cut with a hacksaw. This stock, as it stands, will be too short, so the buttplate is ground flat and a recoil pad added. This will lengthen the stock by as much as an inch.

The small parts, including the trigger, hammer, sear, magazine latch, and others, are cut to shape from flat stock by sawing and milling and finished by filing and sanding. Any holes through these parts should be drilled first and the outline of the parts laid out using the holes as reference points. Make cardboard templates for these parts and, with the hole locations lined up, scribe the outline of the part on the metal.

The sheet metal parts, including the trigger bar, disconnector, and action lock, are cut to shape from 14-gauge sheet metal using the methods described above. Since the sheet metal doesn't contain enough carbon to harden properly, they will require surface, or case hardening. This is easily accomplished using the Kasenit treatment described elsewhere.

The coil springs required can usually be found in hardware stores, auto parts stores, and gunsmith supply houses. I used an M16 hammer spring in this gun, as I have before in a number of gun designs, because it is cheap, dependable, and available. These are advertised by surplus parts suppliers at prices from $1 up, which I consider a bargain.

The magazine latch, or retainer, is fitted easily by first drilling the hinge pin hole through the lower receiver. Then, with the magazine in place, the latch is placed in position with the upper end bearing against the block on the back of the magazine and the hole drilled using the hole through the receiver as a drill bushing. This should require little or no further fitting.

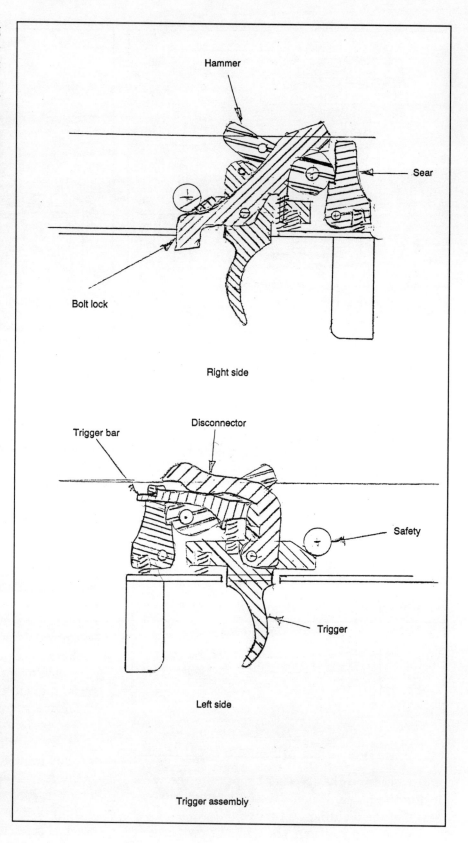

Right side

Left side

Trigger assembly

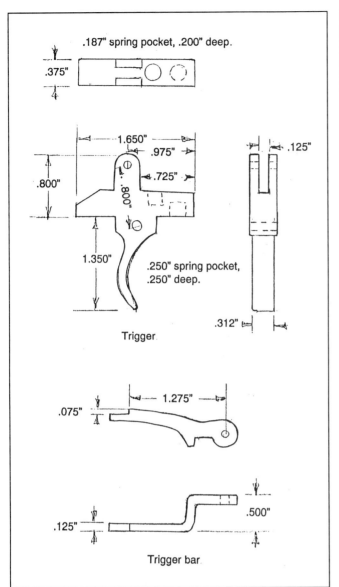

.187" spring pocket, .200" deep.

.375"

1.650"
.975"
.725"
.800"
.800"
1.350"
.125"
.312"

.250" spring pocket, .250" deep.

Trigger

.075"
1.275"
.125"
.500"

Trigger bar

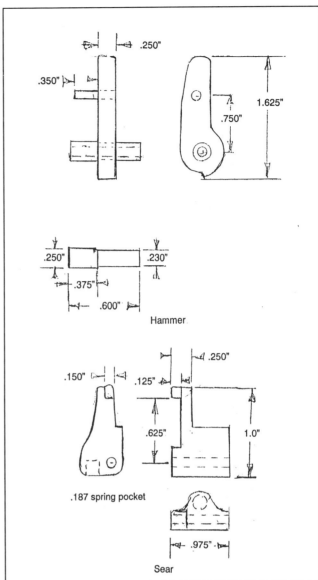

.250"
.350"
1.625"
.750"

.250"
.375"
.230"
.600"

Hammer

.150"
.250"
.125"
.625"
1.0"

.187 spring pocket

.975"

Sear

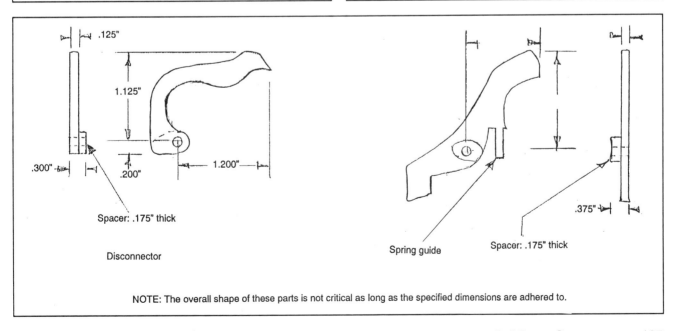

.125"
1.125"
.300"
.200"
1.200"

Spacer: .175" thick

Disconnector

Spring guide

Spacer: .175" thick

.375"

NOTE: The overall shape of these parts is not critical as long as the specified dimensions are adhered to.

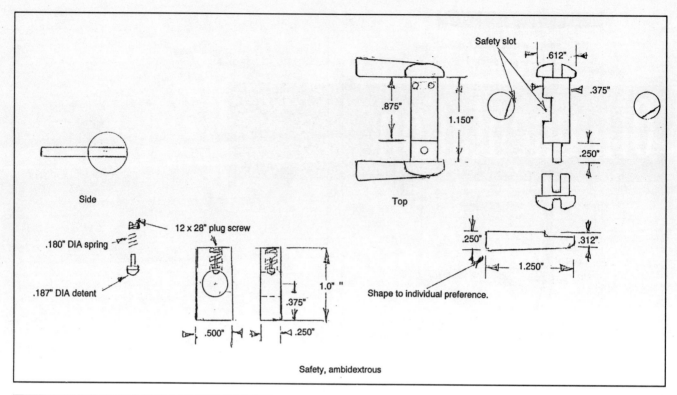

Safety slot

.612"

.375"

.875"

1.150"

.250"

Side

Top

.180" DIA spring

12 x 28" plug screw

.250"

.312"

.187" DIA detent

1.0" "

1.250"

Shape to individual preference.

.375"

.500"

.250"

Safety, ambidextrous

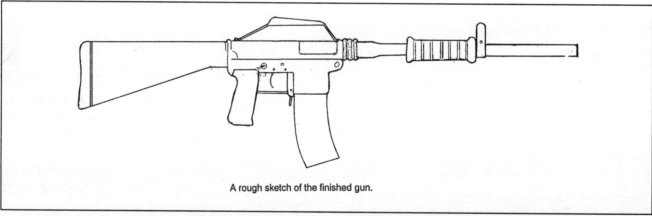

A rough sketch of the finished gun.

A slot is cut with a 1/8-inch end mill in the grip for the rear end of the trigger guard to fit into. The tabs at the front mate into the slots in the lower receiver, forming a solid assembly when the grip is secured in place.

Assembly is accomplished by pinning the sear in place, followed by the hammer. The action lock is then installed, followed by the safety, then the trigger and disconnector, which both pivot on the same pin. The trigger assembly is installed in the lower receiver body, which is then secured to the upper receiver with the crossbolt at the front of the action and the grip bolt at the rear.

Chapter

Ornamentation

17

There are times when, as a number of good guns are displayed together, either standing in racks or laid out on display tables, one among the group will divert attention away from the others. This happens even when the entire group consists of the same make and model. Almost invariably this is due to the one having a better finish. Or maybe more attractive figure or graining in the stock wood. A good bit of the time though, it will be due to extra ornamentation such as engine turning of bright parts, matting and metal checkering, or an outstanding checkering job.

Whatever the reason, the prototype gun that we have spent so much time and effort to produce should be an attention getter. Therefore, we will finish all exposed surfaces to the best of our ability. All metal surfaces are finished free from tool marks and blemishes, with all surfaces flat and true. Lines remain straight and well defined and corners sharp and square. The wood is smooth and without tool or sanding marks, with all pores of the grain filled, and a slick, smooth,

even finish applied. This should be enough to attract and hold anyone's attention. The worst trouble is, most of the others may be equally well finished. So let's take a look at some extra ornamentation that will usually be the attention getter required to make our gun stand out from the others and be noticed first.

Engine turning, also known as damascening and spot polishing, is a type of ornamental polishing used mostly on breech blocks, or bolts, and magazine followers. Properly done, this process adds considerably to the appearance of the finished firearm. It is also handy for covering minor blemishes that cannot be removed easily.

The process consists of overlapping polished circles of small diameter, equally spaced lengthwise and crosswise, or around the circumference of a round bolt. This is normally done using an abrasive-tipped tool chucked in a drill press. These tools can consist of small abrasive-loaded rubber rods, which are usually 3/16 or 1/4 inch in diameter. These are contained in a holder especially made for the purpose and available from gunsmith supply houses. They can also be held in thin-walled tubing or a rod with a hole drilled in one end. The commercial holder doesn't cost much, so it should be used if possible.

Another, better, method is to use small wire brushes of 3/16 or 1/4 inch diameter mounted on a stem that can be secured in a drill chuck. These brushes will begin to spread out as they are used and make a progressively larger pattern. This spreading can be prevented by slipping a tight-fitting O ring or a short length of heat-shrink plastic tubing over the brush, leaving only about 1/8 inch protruding.

Either of these is mounted in a drill chuck and turned at a fairly high speed. The wire brush must be used with an abrasive paste compound mixed with cutting oil. The part to be processed is given a thin coating of the abrasive paste and the wire brush brought into contact with the surface. The wire brush, turning in and coated with the fairly coarse abrasive compound, will make well-defined complete circles on a rounded surface while the solid abrasive rods may not. The rods can also be used with the abrasive paste to give deeper patterns.

It is important that some precise method of spacing be used to obtain a perfect job. If flat surfaces are present, the milling machine can be used for both lengthwise and crosswise spacing. If a round bolt or other part is to be patterned, some sort of indexing fixture should be used. These are also available from gunsmith supply houses and

Sculptured cheek piece, steel grip cap, and fine line checkering add to the attractiveness of this custom rifle.

The grip on this Remington 1100 stock is skip-line checkered.

should be acquired if a number of jobs is anticipated. If only a few will be done, equally spaced index marks can be laid out on masking tape and the tape wrapped around the circumference of the work, as was described elsewhere for indexing muzzle brake gas ports. If care is taken to align these index marks exactly

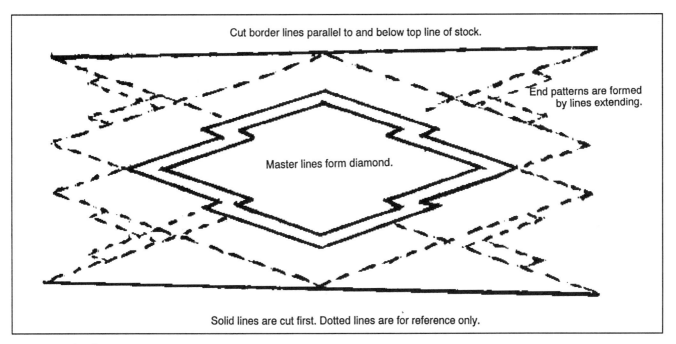

Cut border lines parallel to and below top line of stock.

End patterns are formed by lines extending.

Master lines form diamond.

Solid lines are cut first. Dotted lines are for reference only.

Wraparound point pattern.

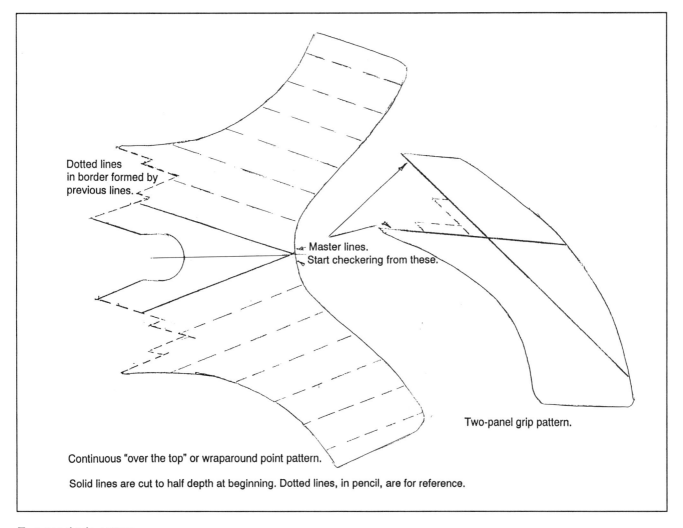

Dotted lines in border formed by previous lines.

Master lines.
Start checkering from these.

Two-panel grip pattern.

Continuous "over the top" or wraparound point pattern.

Solid lines are cut to half depth at beginning. Dotted lines, in pencil, are for reference.

Two-panel grip pattern.

on center in the mill vise, a presentable job can be done.

The appearance of exposed screw heads can be enhanced somewhat by checkering them with a fine metal checkering file. The appearance of these will be improved if true diamonds, approximately three times as long as they are wide, are formed. Short, dumpy diamonds or squares, as many people who try to do this wind up with, are not nearly as attractive as the longer diamonds.

One simple way to do this is to clamp the body of the screw or bolt in a vise with the screw slot at a right angle to the vise jaws. The bottom side of the screw head should rest against the top of the vise. Spaced lines are cut with the checkering file at a 30 degree angle to the screw slot. After the screw head is covered in this one direction, another

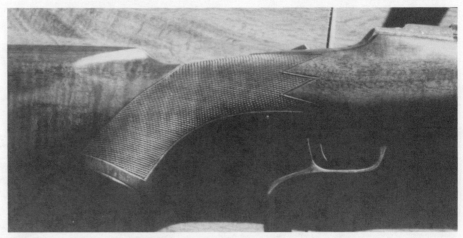

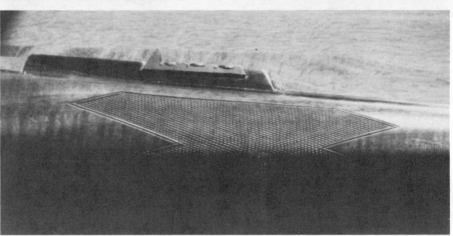

The grip and forend shown here are checkered using a wraparound pattern with border.

set of lines is cut at an opposing matching angle to the screw slot. Several passes will be required to cut the diamonds to their proper depth, which will be the depth required to bring the tops of the diamonds to sharp points. Sometimes it is necessary to use a small triangular file to point up the diamonds.

Matting can be used to both enhance and break up the otherwise plain surfaces and to lessen light reflection. Border lines should first be cut around the perimeter of the area to be matted. Straight, even border lines can be cut lightly into the metal surface by chucking round work in the lathe. A sharp point is ground on one end of a lathe cutting tool, which is then mounted in the lathe tool post with the sharp point exactly on center.

Assume that we are marking border lines that will enclose a matted area on the upper side of a round receiver. Since the receiver is already mounted in the lathe chuck with the outboard

end supported by a center, the sharp, pointed tool is drawn up against the surface of the receiver using the lathe cross slide. Rotate the receiver until the location of the border line is directly in line with the lathe tool. Then feed the tool into the receiver surface lightly with the cross feed and draw it lengthwise using the lathe carriage hand wheel. It is rotated at each end, with the lathe tool still making a light cut, to the point where the other lengthwise border line begins, and it is again drawn lengthwise along the surface. All four corners are connected in this manner.

Borders are cut in the same manner on flat surfaces by forming a sharp point on a short piece of drill rod or a broken end mill, which is then mounted in the milling machine quill. With light down pressure on the pointed tool, cut longitudual lines by drawing the material lengthwise with the handwheel on the milling machine table. The power feed can be used for

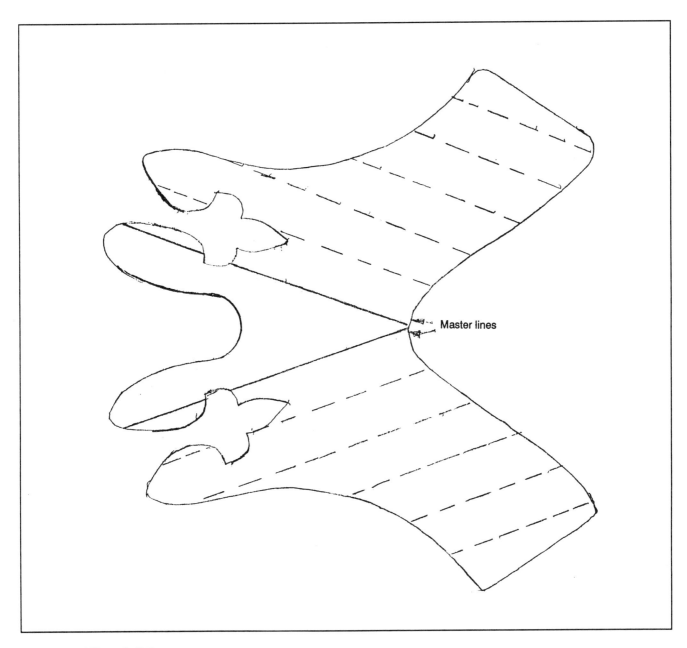

Master lines

Wraparound "fleur-de-lis" pattern.

this. End cuts, or right angle cuts, are made using the crossfeed. Any burrs that are thrown up as a result of this process should be removed before proceeding further.

The actual matting can be done in a number of ways. One way is to make up a matting punch by forming a pattern on a short piece of drill rod. An easy way to form such a pattern is to place one end of the drill rod (it should be 3/16 or 1/4 inch in diameter and some 3 inches long) against a fairly coarse file and hit the other end with a hammer. This will leave an imprint

of the file teeth on the face of the punch. The drill rod is then rotated 90 degrees and the process repeated. This will result in a pattern consisting of small squares on the face. The drill rod is now hardened and drawn at a light straw color. It can now be used like a punch by placing it against the surface of the receiver and hitting it with a hammer. This process is repeated until all the area inside the borders has been covered. Another tool just like this one should be made, but with two flat adjacent sides in order to get completely up to the corners of the border.

An easier, less time-consuming method will result from use of the electric engraving tool that is sold in hardware stores and hobby shops all over the country. These come with a carbide tip installed. If possible, a diamond point should be obtained and installed since it will stay sharp far longer.

To use the tool, turn it on and move the point back and forth across the surface. Some 7,000 to 8,000 strokes per minute will result in a close, evenly matted surface. The material should rest on a solid surface while being treated. If it is held in one hand and the engraving tool held in the other, the finished pattern will take longer to complete because the matted material will tend to bounce away from the engraving tool. The tool has a calibrated stroke adjustment which supposedly regulates the length of the stroke. This should be set first near the middle of its settings and adjusted according to your taste. With a little practice, professional quality work will result.

This treatment can also be applied to sight bases, shotgun ribs, the tops of quarter ribs, and any other surface where contrast or a non-reflective surface is desired. When used on the upper surfaces of certain receivers and the remainder finished in a highly polished bright blue, the lower receiver finished with a vivid case-colored pattern or french grey, combined with well-figured, gloss-finished wood and a decent checkering job, the end result will certainly attract attention.

Like so many other dimensions of craftsmanship, well-executed checkering is the result of understanding what is required to obtain it and practice. Good checkering consists of a series of fine diamonds contained within a border or outline. Each of these diamonds is of equal size and shape. The lines are straight and, if interrupted by a ribbon or other design within the pattern, continue on the other side as though no such interruption was made. All diamonds are cut to the same depth and finished to sharp points all the way up to the border, where the lines forming the checkering stop without any nicks or runovers. The diamonds formed are just that, diamonds. Not squares or rectangles, but true diamonds, with a length of at least three times their width. Equally important, the pattern matches on both sides.

The preceding describes what could be con-

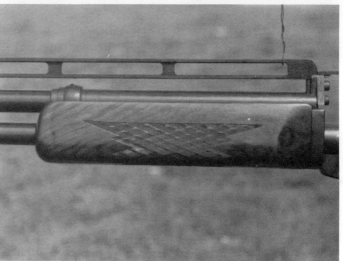

A trap gun stock and forend with skip-line checkering.

sidered a perfect checkering job. One could do well to try to achieve this. In 50 years of trying, I have yet to execute a perfect checkering job. Neither has anyone else that I ever saw. Every job that I have ever examined has had a little something wrong with it, my own included. But we keep trying in the hope that we will, someday, achieve this goal.

As with other undertakings, decent tools and equipment will have a positive effect on the finished product. Checkering tools have come a long way since the time when I tried to use pieces of umbrella rib with teeth filed in as a spacer and a bent triangular file to deepen the lines. I had to hunt for several months before I found a junk umbrella to salvage ribs from.

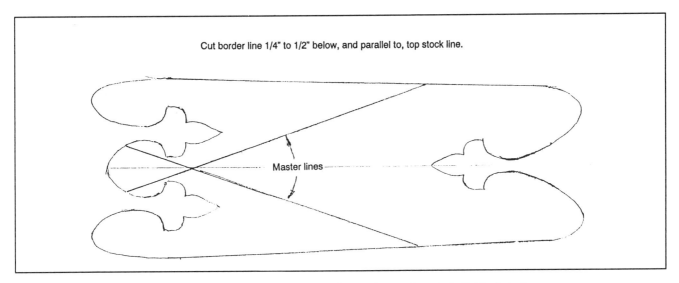

Cut border line 1/4" to 1/2" below, and parallel to, top stock line.

Master lines

Fleur-de-lis wraparound forend pattern. Dimensions must be changed to conform to individual stocks.

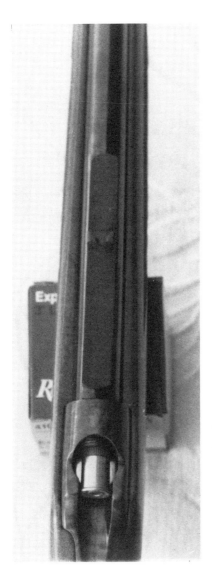

This .410-gauge single-shot shotgun shows a matted quarter rib and case-colored action. This gun was an attention getter.

Today there are several makers of quality checkering tools at reasonable prices. These go a long way toward eliminating the excuse that "I didn't have any good tools." These are generally available as individual tools or in sets. While all the tools that make up a set will eventually come in handy, a two-line spacing tool and a single-line tool are all that are absolutely necessary. A border cutting tool should probably be acquired at the same time, since minor runovers and nicks in the border can be camouflaged using this tool.

My own choice of commercial tools are the handles made by W.E. Brownell, which are called "full view" checkering tools because of a loop in the handle just behind the cutter. The full view feature is not as important as the fact that these handles are stiffer and less subject to bending or springing than the others. I suggest that you purchase four of these handles.

I prefer the cutters made by Dem-Bart. They seem to stay sharp longer than the others, and the spacers tend to be more uniform. It isn't funny to change cutters partway through a checkering job, only to find that the new cutter doesn't cut the same width lines as the one replaced. Several of each cutter should be purchased. Single-line cutters, two-line spacers, a bordering cutter (one of these will last a long time), and a couple of skip-line cutters which will eventually come in handy.

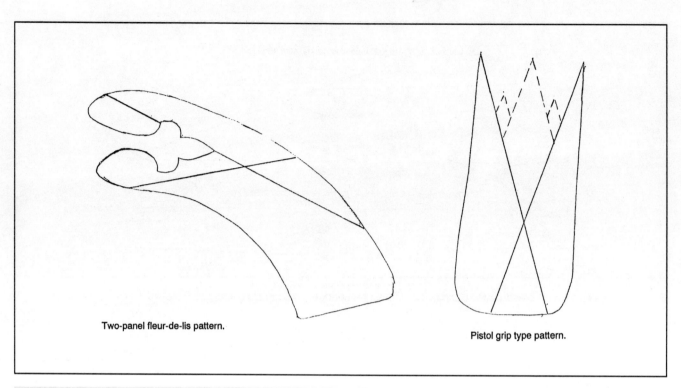

Two-panel fleur-de-lis pattern.

Pistol grip type pattern.

Skip-line checkering is attractive and resistant to wear, and it provides a nonslip surface that is useful on competition guns. It is accomplished by spacing a predetermined number of lines (usually three or four) with the standard fine-line cutter, then one line with a wider spacing tool. This is repeated within the entire pattern.

A small veining tool is needed for cutting tight curves in borders and sometimes for finishing very short lines. Dem-Bart makes one of these and includes it in their checkering sets. The one made by Gunline and sold as an individual tool as well as in their checkering tool sets works better, for me at least. This V tool has a little radius left at the bottom on the inside of the cutting edge. If this radius is removed with a knife edge stone, file, or narrow grinding wheel, the tool will cut smoother and cleaner.

While you are ordering the tools, include a

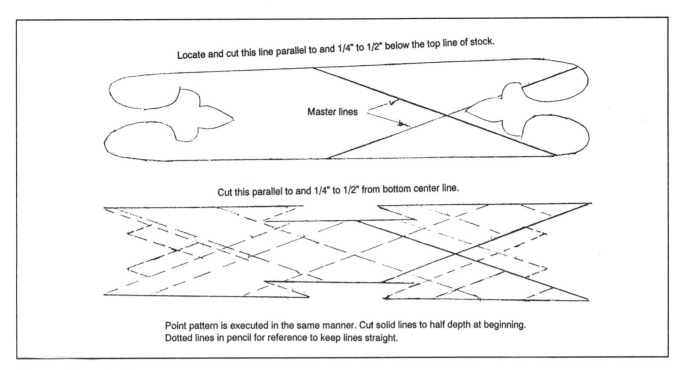

Locate and cut this line parallel to and 1/4" to 1/2" below the top line of stock.

Master lines

Cut this parallel to and 1/4" to 1/2" from bottom center line.

Point pattern is executed in the same manner. Cut solid lines to half depth at beginning.
Dotted lines in pencil for reference to keep lines straight.

Two-panel forend patterns.

Dem-Bart layout guide. This consists of a bent scribing tool fastened to a wood block, with a setscrew to hold it in place. The space between the scriber and the wood block is adjustable. By locking the quill in place and drawing the wood block along the top of the stock, top forend border lines can be located parallel to and exactly the same distance from the top line of the stock.

A good checkering cradle is also a necessity. Do not get one of the cheap ones made from a pine 2 x 4 with a couple of stove bolts holding it together. The people who sell these should be ashamed of themselves. A good commercially made checkering cradle will cost over $100. You can make one yourself that will serve as well as any you could buy, but it should be made from metal or hardwood, not cheap pine. Almost every gun magazine has featured articles on how to build checkering cradles, so it should be a simple matter to find plans for one. The sturdiest design available should be used.

Correct layout of the checkering pattern is one of the most important aspects. Once this is accomplished, you are well on your way to an acceptable job. The biggest problem that can have a diverse effect on this is the fact that many stocks are not symmetrical. There was a time when I took in custom checkering jobs on stocks

that others had made. Most of these were made, or I should say finished, from semi-inletted blanks. Almost invariably, they were lopsided, or nonsymmetrical, or thicker on one side than the other. By cheating, I usually managed to get most patterns to appear the same on both sides. But if anyone had taken the trouble to measure, they would have found that each panel differed in direct proportion to how much the stock varied from side to side.

Two more items should be made before beginning. A plastic diamond, 3 inches long and 1 inch wide, is cut from thin, clear plastic sheet. A visible center line should be scribed, both lengthwise and crosswise. This will serve as a template to establish the angle of the master lines in each panel and assures that they will all be similar.

One or more strips, 1/2 inch wide and at least 8 inches long, can be cut from the same material. Both sides of these should be straight, smooth, and parallel. These will be used to lay out the full-length master lines by wrapping them around the stock at the established angle and drawing a line alongside.

A centerline must be established along the bottom side of the forend. This would be simple enough if we were sure it was symmetrical.

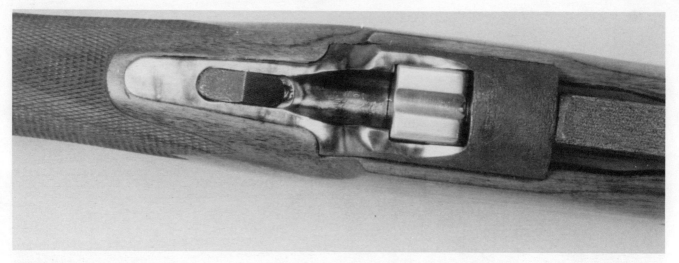

Wraparound checkering goes over the top of the grip without interruption. The matted quarter rib and receiver top are also visible, as is the case-colored receiver. Care must be taken to keep the lines even and the spacing tool held perpendicular to the stock's surface; otherwise the diamonds will change shape as the job progresses. Parallel reference lines should be drawn some 1/2" apart inside the area to be checkered. This will assist in keeping lines straight.

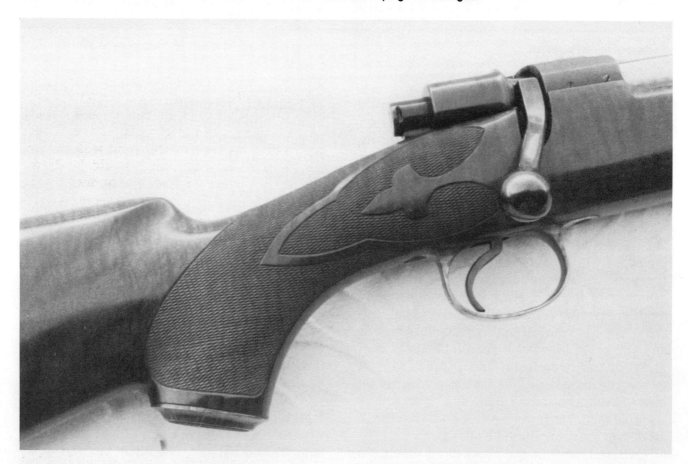

Fleur-de-lis checkering done by the author several years ago. Note that the lines continue in the same direction after crossing the ribbon and that all diamonds are approximately the same size and shape. I consider this a fairly good job, but still far from perfect.

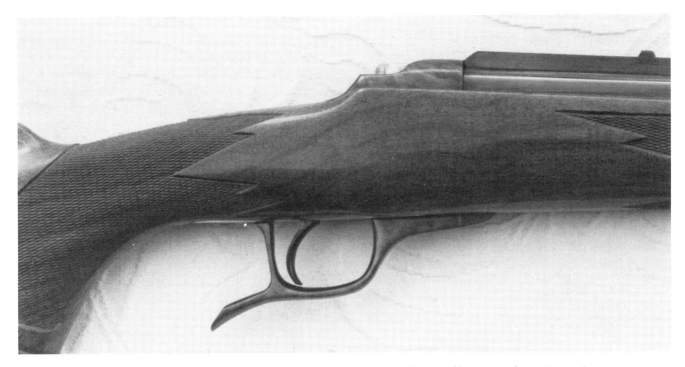

A point pattern of "recessed" or "inset" checkering whereby the area to be checkered is recessed or cut away to a predetermined depth before the checkering is done. This is not really worth the extra effort involved.

Simply wrap a piece of paper around it and mark both outside edges. Fold the paper in half, then wrap it around the stock again. The crease where it was folded will indicate the centerline. Since it probably isn't symmetrical, however, this won't work. Pad the sides with thin cardboard or plastic to prevent its being marred or blemished, and draw up a parallel clamp snug against the sides, just behind the forend tip. Measure across the jaws and halve the measurement. Mark it on the stock. This will be the forward end of the centerline. Move the clamp to the rear just ahead of the action and repeat the operation. A lengthwise line connecting these two points will be the exact centerline. The line should be drawn with a very soft pencil on a piece of masking tape positioned lengthwise along the bottom of the forend.

The upper border lines are scribed using the layout guide as described earlier. Make sure these are the same length and begin at the same point. If the forend pattern is to wrap completely around the wood, the plastic diamond is positioned on the centerline and a line drawn along two sides, forming the angle of the master lines. These lines are extended to the borders by placing the long plastic strip along the angle lines and extending them with a pencil. If a

two-piece pattern is used, lower border lines are drawn on each side of, parallel to, and equally spaced along the bottom centerline. These drawn lines are then carefully cut with the single-line tool. Adjacent lines should be drawn parallel to the master lines and spaced by the width of the plastic strips. These serve as reference points to aid in keeping the spaced lines pointing in the same direction. If curved end borders are to be used, they should be located using a template or pattern and the outline drawn. If a point pattern is used, the outline is drawn with a soft pencil only and the final outline established by the checkering.

We hear about making paper patterns and wrapping them around the grip. This won't really work since the paper won't conform to the compound curves of the lower side of the grip. This is still a good idea if you can come up with ductile material for the pattern that will conform to the contour without wrinkling. A thin sheet of lead big enough for the pattern would be ideal for this. With a line drawn at the desired distance above and parallel to the grip cap to serve as a locating point and a centerline drawn along the top of the grip, the sheet lead pattern is positioned in place and a line drawn around it. It is then repositioned on the other side and the process repeated. Master lines are located and drawn using the plastic diamond.

The stock is mounted in the checkering cradle and the actual checkering begun by placing one row of the spacing tools' teeth in one of the master lines and moving it firmly back and forth, cutting from one border to the other. No attempt should be made to cut the lines to full depth on this first pass; we are only spacing the lines. Cut each line up to the border and stop. The cutter must be held perpendicular to the surface of the stock through the entire length of the cut. If it is allowed to tilt or angle either way, the line spacing will be affected. This is one of the main advantages of using the cradle, since the work can be rotated under the cutter. When both master lines have been paralleled on both sides with spaced lines and the entire pattern filled in, the single-line cutter is used to deepen the lines and bring the dia-monds to a point. The lines will require going over several times, both with the single-line tool and at least one more pass with the spacing tool, when the lines are almost to full depth. This will serve to keep the line width uniform. Remember to always hold the cutter perpendicular to the work.

Finish the work by cutting the outline to full depth. If you have runovers, the border tool should be used to cut a two-line border which, hopefully, will hide them. If they are bad enough that two lines didn't hide them, you might as well cut another border around the whole business, and let on like you admire wide borders.

When the checkering is as good as you can make it, brush it out carefully and completely. A thin coat of finish is brushed in as an attempt to weatherproof it. Brush it in thoroughly, since any excess that might remain will clog and obscure the pattern.

Chapter

Fitting and Assembly

18

With all the component parts made, we are now faced with the task of putting them together in a manner that will cause the gun to look and perform in a way that makes us proud.

If slots for the extractor(s) have not yet been cut in the bolthead, it should be done now. The spring pockets are drilled and, with the extractor in place, a hole for the hinge pin is drilled. The hook engages the rim of the case when the casehead is held against the bolt face. If an inside extractor is used, it should not have a sharp hook. The case rim must cam this one open as the ejector pushes the case out of the action. Try a 60-degree angle first, and modify it if necessary. The extractors should hold the case firmly against the bolt face. Front faces of the extractor hooks should be angled and the edges beveled or rounded to assure that they will slip over the rim of a chambered case.

Clearance for the extractors must be provided, both in the end of the barrel and in the receiver or barrel extension. Relief cuts in the barrel must not extend into the chamber. These cuts should be angled inward, toward the chamber end, and match the angle of the extractor's forward edge closely. Location of these relief cuts can be established by coating the forward edges of the extractors with lipstick or some other form of nondrying colored substance. Then, with both the barrel and bolt in their respective locations in the receiver, the bolt is pushed forward into contact with the end of the barrel. The marks left on the end of the barrel indicate where the relief slots should begin. It may be necessary to remove one extractor when doing this. Locate and fit each one individually. If a rotating bolt is used as a means to lock the action, the slots must continue around the barrel to match the amount of bolt rotation.

Relief must also be provided on the inside of the receiver or barrel extension to allow clearance for the extractors to move outward far enough to slip over the rim of a chambered case. Location of these cuts can also be established through use of a colored compound as described.

The ejector is located on the opposite side,

away from the ejection port. It must extend inside the outer rim of the bolt face, far enough to strike the case head dependably and push (perhaps knock would be a better word) it out of the ejection port with absolute certainty. The ejector is usually attached to the lower frame by use of pins, screws, or silver solder. When assembled to the upper receiver, the ejector must extend up through the bottom of the upper receiver and ride in the slot that has been cut in the bolt to provide clearance for it. It must fit the slot closely but without rubbing or binding.

In an ideal situation, the ejector will contact the casehead, causing the fired case to be thrown out of the gun just as soon as the case mouth will clear the end of the barrel. Since the bottom of the bolt is in contact with the top cartridge in the magazine and is holding it down somewhat, preventing it from interfering with the case being extracted, the fired case must be ejected before the bolt travels far enough to release the next cartridge in the magazine and let it move upward into its feeding position. The forward end of the ejector may have to be cut back further if the case mouth does not clear the end of the barrel. This should be determined by test firing.

Firearms chambered for pistol and .22 rimfire cartridges should have the top of the magazine positioned at a point where the extracting case just clears the magazine lips. We hear about magazine-fed guns having a "straight line feed," but this is mostly another old wives tale. If the magazine is positioned to allow a straight-line feed in, it will also be a straight line back out again, and the head of the extracting case will hit the magazine lips, preventing ejection. Neither the magazine lips nor the next cartridge in the magazine must be allowed to contact the extracted case before it is ejected.

Most of the guns that I have built, except shotguns, utilized the lower side of the ejector to contact the top of the magazine and stop its upward travel. It is held in position by a magazine latch, which, when depressed, allows removal of the magazine. The latch can be quickly and accurately located in position by first drilling the hinge pin hole through both sides of the frame. As usual, the hole through one side is slightly smaller than the other to serve as a means of holding the hinge pin in place. The magazine is then inserted into the frame, or well, and held in place by small wooden wedges between the magazine body and the frame. The magazine latch is placed in the frame with the upper end pushed up tight against whatever it is supposed to bear against, whether it be a block, slot, or notch. Pull the bottom part away from the magazine slightly to approximate the latched position. Then, holding it upward against the latching surface, place it under a drill mounted in a drill press or milling machine quill and drill through the magazine latch. The latch should now be polished on the sides to assure that it doesn't bind and pinned in place with the stiffest coil spring possible inserted in the spring pocket and bearing against the magazine housing. It should latch and hold the magazine in place with little or no up and down movement.

If something slipped while you were drilling the hole and the latch won't snap in place, you should file a little off the top, trying it frequently until it does. If it moved the other way and is too loose, you can make another part, plug the pin hole, and re-drill it, or peen the sides just behind the latching surface, which should stretch the metal enough to tighten the fit. One other way is to build it up slightly by welding and cut it back until it fits.

An ideal firing pin will extend all the way through the bolt, and when the base of the firing pin (the end the hammer contacts) is flush with the rear end of the bolt, the firing pin tip will protrude from the bolt face from .045 to .060 inch. This can be measured using a depth micrometer, if care is taken to hold the base parallel to the bolt face. Centerfire rifle and pistol firing pins should have a tip diameter no larger than .065 inch. Shotgun diameters are somewhat larger, anywhere from .100 to .125 inch. Whatever the diameter, any of these should fit the hole through the bolt face closely and have a hemispherical, or half rounded, tip.

The firing pin is held in place inside the bolt by a crosspin that intersects the firing pin hole at approximately one fourth of its diameter. The larger base end is relieved to clear this crosspin, which should permit some .150 inch of lengthwise movement. The crosspin hole can be located anywhere around the circumference of the bolt, as long as it doesn't interfere with the function of any other parts. It should be 3/8 inch from the rear of the bolt and drilled off center from the firing pin hole, whereby only about half the diameter of the crosspin protrudes into the firing pin hole. When drilling the hole, it must be plugged with a close-fitting rod to support the drill as it intersects the firing pin hole. If this is not done, the drill will try to "crawl," or wander off to the unsupported side and probably break. Hold the rod that is used to plug the hole with vise grips or some other kind of clamp to prevent its turning when the drill contacts it.

One side of the firing pin must be relieved to clear the crosspin. The easiest way to cut it is with a 1/8-inch end mill. A coil spring that fits inside the firing pin hole without binding and is strong enough to keep the firing pin retracted inside the bolt body except when the hammer pushes it forward is inserted in the firing pin hole. The firing pin is installed with the relief cut lined up with the crosspin hole and the crosspin put in place. Make sure that the firing pin moves back and forth without binding.

The firing pin tip protrusion, as applied to the striker-fired bolt, is stopped by contact between the cocking piece and the cocking cam. Protrusion is adjusted by screwing the threaded firing pin in or out until the correct protrusion is achieved.

Particular care must be taken when fitting the trigger group parts. Dummy pins, longer than the actual assembly pins, are made up so that the parts can be assembled on the outside of the frame or housing. The longer pins are placed in their respective pin holes and the component parts assembled on these pins in their appropriate locations. This will enable you to observe and establish the correct angles for the sear and hammer notches.

The sear nose and hammer notch should be square with each other when the hammer is in the cocked position. If the hammer notch is cut at a steeper angle, pulling or pushing the sear out of engagement will require it to cam the hammer back against the hammer spring slightly, which will result in an excessively heavy trigger pull. If the angle of the notch is shallow, it can be jarred off the sear, sometimes simply by the impact of the bolt slamming shut. This is an accidental way to make a full-automatic weapon. It is also unsafe since it will probably fire when you don't want it to.

If a trigger bar is used to transfer trigger movement to the sear, the length of it can also be determined closely by using this mockup assembly system. There must be a clearance of .005 to .010 inch between the trigger bar and sear to assure that the bar will re-engage with the sear after being cammed out of engagement by the disconnector. Too much clearance will result in excessive trigger travel. The disconnector proper should bear against the trigger bar and cam it out of engagement with the sear as the bolt retracts. The cam that causes disengagement must be located directly behind the rear end of the bolt, with just enough clearance to permit it to engage when the bolt is closed completely. Rearward movement of the bolt should immediately disconnect the trigger, preventing firing unless the bolt is fully forward and locked.

As used in the slide-action gun, an action lock is required. This locks the action closed until the trigger is pulled. Then, a pin in the right side of the hammer contacts the locking bar and pushes it downward and out of engagement with the rear end of the bolt, thereby allowing the bolt to be moved to the rear. The portion of this lock that contacts the bolt, preventing rearward movement, should have just enough clearance to assure that its normal movement will not be impeded. It should extend upward only enough to lock positively. The release lever located just behind the trigger is pushed upward to manually disengage the lock, permitting loading and unloading. This part will probably require a considerable amount of hand fitting and trying, especially on your first gun.

The sliding safety, located just ahead of the trigger, is in what most people who have used one consider the most accessible position possible. Formerly favored by the U.S. military and used in both the M1 and M14 rifles since it was equally accessible to both left- and right-handed shooters, it was moved to other locations in succeeding models that required a selector switch to permit full-automatic fire incorporated with the safety.

The safety, as used here, requires that a flange at the front end of the slide body slips under the lower end of the sear, locking it into the hammer notch. The flange should be beveled slightly at each end, which will permit it to start under the sear easily and, with further travel, cam it forward slightly. There must be very little slack between these two parts. Two shallow dimples are formed on the bottom side of the trigger housing. A 1/8-inch drill can be used to do this. A spring-loaded detent contained in the body of the safety engages the dimples, preventing movement unless manipulated by hand. These must be positioned so that they engage at each end of the safety's travel.

It is fairly important that the chamber be cut within the prescribed headspace limits. When using a blowback action for centerfire cartridges, the chamber should be cut with little or no headspace. Even a chamber that is .005 to .010 inch less than standard depth is acceptable. The .22 rimfire must have a full-depth chamber whereby the bolt will close completely on a .043 inch rim thickness. If the .22 chamber is too shallow, the impact of a semiautomatic bolt closing can very well crush the rim enough to detonate the priming compound and cause unintentional firing of the gun. I have had this happen.

Locked-breech guns using high-pressure centerfire cartridges should have chambers cut to prescribed dimensions, using standard headspace gauges if possible. Shims of .006 to .008 inch can be used with factory cartridges if no gauges are available. Shotgun shells vary in dimension a good bit, so slide-action and autoloading guns can have a chamber where the bolt will close on a shim .010 inch thick placed between the shell head and the bolt face. Bolt-action guns can be slightly tighter.

Correct chamber depth can be determined by installing the bolt in its locked position in the receiver or barrel extension. The distance between the bolt face and the forward edge of the receiver or barrel extension is measured using a depth micrometer. The chamber should be cut until this same measurement, less .005 or .006 inch, is reached by measuring from a chambered factory dimensioned casehead to the shoulder of the barrel just in front of the threads. If the barrel has an integral approach cone, the distance between the end of the approach cone and the shoulder which contacts the receiver should be measured. This measurement will be longer than the measurement taken from the bolt face to the receiver end, so we subtract the smaller from the larger. This distance, plus a few thousandths, say .005 inch, should be the depth

to a chambered casehead, as measured from the end of the approach cone. These measurements will not be absolute, since thread stretching, shoulders crushing, and pure sloppiness may affect them. But they will be close.

The angled approach cone as used in the 03 Springfield and the M54 and M70 Winchesters contribute to flawless feeding. Several years ago, certain manufacturers announced revolutionary discoveries concerning tighter breeching which, supposedly, rendered this system obsolete. Actually what they did was fix something that wasn't broken. Now, several designers have rediscovered the old system and adopted it as their own. And with good reason—this is the most foolproof system devised so far. Every now and then, some so-called "gunmaker" announces that he has made a major improvement by changing the approach cone angle by a degree or so. Regardless of what they may claim, a 45-degree angle will serve as well as any.

The feeding of rimmed cartridges or shells can be improved by using a slightly convex contour in the approach cone. When the correct shape is arrived at, it will guide the end of the shell or cartridge past the rim counterbore in the end of the chamber without the scraping and gouging sometimes experienced.

The high rear sight base/carrying handle combinations should have short tabs bent parallel to the receiver and the horizontal part of the carrying handle. A 3/8-inch hole is drilled through each of these. With the base and receiver clamped together in their respective positions, the rims around the two holes are welded, inside to the receiver using a TIG welding process. The holes should be filled and the welds built up slightly above the surface and dressed back flush with the surface of the surrounding metal. The edges should be peened down against the receiver with a hammer. This will result in the neatest installation possible. The machined sight bases should be attached with silver solder.

With most of the designs described in this book, the barrel assembly is held in place in the receiver by a knurled retaining nut which screws onto the front end of the receiver. The buttstock is secured to the lower receiver by means of a through bolt. The telescoping stock is installed in the same manner, except that the inside part must be installed first and the outer buttstock added. The lower receiver, with the trigger assembly contained inside it, is attached to the upper and held in place by one or more bolts. The bolt at the rear will extend through the grip and hold it in place.

Shotgun muzzle brakes are assembled by first installing the locknut on the rear threaded collar. The main body is then installed and turned into place on this same threaded collar. The front part of the brake is then installed on the front threaded collar and turned, or screwed, up tight against the body of the brake, with the flange on the outer rim of the front part inside the body. If the front sight is mounted on the brake body, it should be turned to its approximate position and locked in place with the locknut. Final determination of the sight's position will be determined by firing and adjusting until the desired point of impact is found.

One last important point that must not be overlooked is the installation of a locating pin to position the barrel assembly in the same relationship to the receiver when it is removed and replaced. A 1/8 inch wide slot is cut through the wall of the upper receiver, extending back from the front edge 1/2 inch. With the barrel positioned in place, and using the slot as a guide, a No. 31 drill is used to drill a hole for the locating pin into the surface of the barrel. Do not drill all the way through the barrel. A short 1/8-inch diameter pin is pressed into the hole and shortened until the barrel retaining nut will screw in place over it. This pin and slot relationship will relocate the barrel assembly in the same position each time it is assembled.

Chapter

Firing and Adjusting

19

Whether we like it or not, very few prototype firearms function flawlessly when first assembled. Some of the ones that I built wouldn't shoot at all until I redesigned and rebuilt them slightly.

With all of the component parts heat treated and finished, the gun should be assembled and tested before bluing. This is done because a certain amount of file work and further polishing may be required which would mar the finish and cause it to have to be redone. This is, generally, a waste of time.

Before any attempt is made to fire the gun, you should make certain that the chamber and bore are clean and free from abrasive dust and metal cuttings. Make sure that a cartridge or shell will go all the way into the chamber and come out again without effort. If it doesn't, something is wrong. You should have been using a new unblemished factory round for the test. Inspect it carefully for scratches or burrs made by whatever interfered with its chambering. A sharp edge at the lip of the chamber or burrs

along the extractor slots will likely be the cause. A small amount of polishing may very well cure the problem. Sometimes it is necessary to insert the chamber reamer and turn it a couple of revolutions without any forward pressure exerted.

Headspace should be rechecked after final assembly. When parts are disassembled and put back together again, they sometimes do not fit exactly the way they did the first time. Threads sometimes stretch or shoulders crush during tightening, causing a barrel to extend slightly further into the receiver than it did before. This can cause a decrease in headspace.

Headspace, to anyone who doesn't know, has nothing to do with hat size. It is the distance between the head of a fully chambered case and the face of the breechblock, or bolt. Since rim thickness and cartridge lengths, which establish headspace, are not always identical, the chamber must be cut deep enough to allow the bolt to close on all standard cartridges of the specific caliber. Since it is sometimes difficult to tell which are the largest or smallest cartridges in a given caliber, headspace gauges should be used to come up with the correct chamber depth if possible. Otherwise, thin shims should be used between the cartridge head and the bolt face. The bolt should not close on a shim over .006 inch thick. Several cartridges should be tried along with the shim, and the bolt should close on them all. If the headspace is excessive, the easiest cure is to set the barrel back one thread and recut the chamber to the correct depth.

I have been reading and hearing about what will result from firing guns with excessive headspace ever since I was a boy. Several of the older gun books warn of actions being blown into small pieces due to this condition. I have never seen this happen. I have seen blown-up actions and pistol cylinders as well as blown-out chambers on shotgun barrels a number of times. But excessive headspace was not the cause. Extreme overloads, overlong case necks, and the wrong powder were the causes. I have never seen a blown-up gun caused by factory ammunition. If one uses factory loads exclusively, few problems will be experienced.

An example comes to mind that lends credibility to the idea that excessive headspace is not as dangerous as many people believe. It must have been 30 years ago when a couple of acquaintances came to my shop with an old 1893 7mm Mauser. They said they had been trying to blow it up by using various overloads. They said they had tied the gun to a truck tire and pulled the trigger with a long string. They claimed to have fired over 500 rounds of the hottest ammunition they could concoct through this gun. The only damage to the gun was to set the bolt back enough to result in about .050 inch of excessive headspace. They needed an extra gun to hunt with the next day and wanted to know if there was anything I could do to assure that it would be safe to shoot.

I didn't really want to, but I peened the locking lugs enough to move the rear edges back far enough to eliminate the excessive headspace. We agreed that it should only be fired a few times and that I was not to be held responsible for any mishaps that might occur. I lost track of the owner and the gun some 15 years ago, but the last I knew he was still using it and it was still in one piece. So it may be that the horror tales we hear regarding excessive headspace are some-what exaggerated. This is not to say that I endorse excessive headspace. Nothing could be further from the truth. I always have and will continue to set up chambers within the prescribed limits. But I am sure that many thousands of rounds are fired each year from firearms with excessive headspace without the disastrous results predicted.

The first time the gun is tried, an empty case containing a primer only should be loaded and fired. If an autoloader, the bolt should be allowed to slam shut on the chambered case. A slide-action should have the bolt jerked forward as rapidly as possible. If the firing pin is too long or protrudes too far, this is a good way to find out. If the hammer can be jarred out of engagement, you need to know about it before you start using live ammunition. When firing primers only, you will find that the primer backs out of the case slightly. This is normal and nothing to be concerned about, since the impact of the firing pin pushes the case forward into the chamber. This does not happen with loaded rounds since gas pressure pushes the case back against the bolt face.

If the empty case and primer test works out as it should—that is, if the primer does not fire until the trigger is pulled—a live round should be fired. Use a factory-loaded round for this. Of course your handloads are better than factory rounds, but why waste them when an inferior factory-loaded round can be used in its place?

How much confidence you have in your ability should govern the method you use to test fire the gun. Ever since I have been old enough to know what was going on, I have heard about gunsmiths tying newly rebarreled or otherwise modified guns to some heavy object and test firing them by means of a heavy string attached to the trigger. I have personally built, manufactured, rebarreled, and otherwise modified several thousand guns in my lifetime, and I have never once felt it necessary to resort to remote-control firing such as this. While I do usually hold each gun at arms length and in one hand to test fire it, this is mostly because I don't want gas in my face in the event that the firing pin should be longer than I thought it was and pierces the primer. In my own guns, I have verified that the bore, chamber, locking system, and materials used are the way they are supposed to be. There is no reason to even think they might blow up. This is not to say that I recommend your doing likewise. You must make up your own mind as to how you handle it. Personally, I would not take the chance of having my gun skinned up or otherwise marred if the tied-down gun kicks loose from its mounting and goes skidding along the ground or other hard surface.

After the first round is fired, pay close attention to whether or not the case extracts and ejects easily. If the empty case is not extracted, there may be any of several reasons. With an autoloading action, it often happens that the bolt doesn't open far enough for the ejector to contact the casehead. When this happens, the empty case simply goes back in the chamber when the bolt closes. This will make it appear that the case didn't extract, so check it further by pulling the bolt briskly to the rear by hand. If the case comes with it and is ejected, we know that something else is wrong.

In the case of a blowback action, there are three things that are likely to cause this: the bolt is too heavy, the recoil spring is too stiff, or the action is too tight to work freely. This is usually due to burrs, toolmarks, or an oversize bolt. Before going any further, remove the recoil spring and work the action back and forth several times by hand. It should reciprocate easily without binding. If it doesn't, take the bolt out and examine it carefully for gouges or scratch marks. If such are present, locate and eliminate the cause, which will usually be a burr or other rough place inside the receiver. It sometimes happens that the bolt needs a slight reduction in diameter to work smoothly. Often this can be accomplished simply by further polishing.

When, and if, the gun works freely, reassemble it and shoot it again. If it still doesn't work, try cutting a couple of coils off the recoil spring and test fire it again. If it still doesn't work, cut a couple more coils. Remember, though, that the recoil spring must retain enough energy to push the bolt forward again while stripping a cartridge from the magazine and pushing it into the chamber, so shortening the spring must not be overdone.

If it still doesn't open completely, weight must be removed from the bolt. Since we can't shorten it without relocating the hammer and firing pin, the best way to remove weight will be by cutting a series of flutes lengthwise around the circumference of the bolt. It is also possible to drill lengthwise holes into the bolt from the back, but care must be taken not to drill into other parts. Keep in mind while doing this that a 9mm blowback bolt should weigh at least 10 ounces, preferably more. A .22 rimfire bolt should weigh at least 4 ounces. A .45 bolt should be a minimum of 12 ounces.

Locked-breech autoloading guns that don't open completely can sometimes be made operative by further polishing as described above. They will seldom need the recoil spring cut or the bolt lightened. Usually they will need the gas ports enlarged or moved closer to the chamber. Make sure the locking surfaces are smooth and lock and unlock without binding.

Manually operated guns will have no such problems. If they or the autoloader fail to eject empty cases, it will usually be because the nose of the empty case strikes or rubs against the edge of the ejection port or the end of the barrel. What happens then is the empty case is knocked back inside the receiver ahead of the extractor, jamming the action. Finding the exact spot where the case hits can be made easier by marking the case so that you know where the top was in relation to the chamber. This can be done with a dot of fingernail polish or lacquer. It can also be marked with a knife or file. Give the edges of the ejection port a coat of lipstick. Close the bolt on the chambered case and retract it as quickly as possible. The point where the case contacts the ejection port should show up, both in the lipstick coating and by a trace of the lipstick on the empty case. The port is enlarged slightly in the area where the case hits. If it hits on the end of the barrel, the ejector can be shortened slightly.

The extractor should have a sharp right-angle hook long enough to engage the rim all the way to the bottom of the rim groove. It must have a heavy enough spring to hold the cartridge base firmly against the bolt face. When so-called dual extractors are used, only the one adjacent to the ejection port actually has a steep hook. The inside one isn't actually an extractor at all but serves to hold the case against the true extractor. This one must have an angled face which will cam open as the ejector strikes the casehead. It too should have a strong spring. When a casehead is caught between the two of these, it should be nearly impossible to pull the case straight forward from between them. It should only pull away when angled toward the outside extractor. The hook angles on the extractors can also cause faulty ejection.

With the chamber empty and the firing mechanism cocked, the gun should be bumped heavily against a sandbag or similar nonrigid surface. This should be done several times, both with the safety engaged and in the firing position. If the hammer or firing mechanisms jars off, the sear and hammer angles must be changed. Don't allow this to go unattended. You should also try to pull the trigger with the safety engaged. This should also be attempted while bumping the gun against the sandbag. If the hammer should fall even once, corrective action must be taken.

The flange at the front of the safety that slides under the tail of the sear and blocks any downward movement must fit closely when engaged. If the hammer can be released with the safety engaged, it indicates that there is excessive clearance between the two parts. This could be corrected temporarily by bending the safety flange upward slightly. The trouble with this is that in time it will probably bend back again, so either a new safety or a new sear must be made with thicker, closer-fitting locking surfaces. Do not neglect this. It could very well get someone hurt or killed in the future.

Locked-breech guns should be checked carefully to make sure the disconnector cams the trigger out of engagement when the bolt is not locked. This can be checked by retracting the bolt about 1/4 inch. The trigger should now move to the rear without releasing the hammer. This is a safety feature to prevent the gun from firing when the breech isn't locked. It is not to prevent full-automatic fire, as some people seem to believe, since full-automatic fire is not possible anyway unless additional parts are added. As it exists here, even if the disconnector was totally removed and the trigger held to the rear, no automatic fire would result. The hammer would simply follow the bolt forward without firing. But if it happened to fire without being locked, the bolt would open prematurely, allowing the unsupported case to be blown apart, spraying bits and particles of the case out of the ejection port. I had this happen once when a guy loaded one of his junk oversized reloads into

one of my shotguns and fired it. It didn't hurt the gun, but someone standing next to the ejection port could have been hurt. With the designs shown in this book, the firing pin is too short to fire the primer unless the bolt is completely locked, or supposed to be. So don't take chances. Make certain that it functions properly.

A cam at the front edge of the disconnector is forced downward by the bolt moving to the rear. This cam must almost contact the rear end of the bolt when in the locked position. If the cam is too short, it will not disengage the trigger until the bolt has opened far enough to unlock. The only way to correct this is to make a new disconnector with the cam further forward and cut it back a little at a time until it works correctly.

The blowback actions don't actually depend on the disconnector for anything except to make it necessary to release the trigger between shots. But it won't have any detrimental effect if these, too, are kept disconnected until the bolt is almost closed.

Very well, we now have the gun to a point where the disconnector works the way it is supposed to and the trigger and safety function properly. The gun will fire and eject an empty case. It is time to check for feeding problems. Place two rounds in the magazine and cycle the action. If the first round feeds and chambers, fire it. If it extracts and feeds the second round, fire it too. If this one also ejects, congratulations, you are almost finished. Try it with several rounds and then a full magazine. If it feeds, fires, and ejects the empty cases, any finish polishing that is required and the bluing should be done. It is finished.

You are probably luckier than I ever was. The .22s I made usually wouldn't feed the first time around, and I wound up bending the magazine lips, and sometimes the follower, until they did feed. A lot of this was caused by the magazines being slightly different, even though they came from the same manufacturer. My 9mms and .45s usually fed as assembled with only an occasional lip adjustment required. My centerfire rifles sometimes needed slight changes in the feed ramp angle to feed properly.

It was the shotguns that gave the most trouble in their early stages. The first shotgun that I built was finally modified and adjusted to a point that it would fire and eject one round. When two rounds were placed in the magazine, it wouldn't eject the first round but would the second. This was after I dug out the first case, which was still in the partially open action but jammed between the end of the barrel and the bolt face, and let it feed the second round. I finally figured out that the nose of the round that was still in the magazine rode too high and pushed the extracted case up against the roof of the receiver, binding it enough to prevent ejection. I reshaped the follower and bent the magazine lips inward at the front, which lowered the nose of the case as it related to the magazine.

After several attempts, I managed to get it right, and it worked perfectly with five shells or less. The shell noses dipped as more shells were added, and with more than five it wouldn't feed anymore. I built a curved magazine, which presented all 10 shells in the same attitude for feeding. This fed all 10 shells perfectly when the action was cycled by hand, but when I shot it, the action wouldn't open all the way if seven or more shells were in the magazine.

I eventually figured out that the shells rubbing against the bottom of the bolt created too much friction as extra shells were added. So I dropped the magazine 1/8 inch. Now none of the shells would feed; they struck the end of the feed ramp. So I cut the feed ramp deeper. Finally the gun worked like I wanted it to, but by now it was so beat up and mutilated that I was ashamed to show it to anyone. I put it in the closet and built another gun. This one—an autoloading gun—worked the first time it was assembled. You won't have most of these problems with manually operated guns. Bending the magazine lips will correct most feeding problems that you may encounter.

Regardless of how well the gun performs, it isn't good for much unless it shoots where the sights point. If adjustable sights are used, it is a simple matter to sight the gun in. But if the simple fixed metallic sights are used, as is common on shotguns and assault type pistols, they must be cut to the heights required to cause them to coincide with where the bullet strikes.

Shoot the gun at a target. If it shoots to the right or left, move the rear sight in the direction that the point of impact is to be moved. If the gun shoots to the right, the rear sight must be moved to the left until it shoots to the point of aim. If it shoots too high, the rear sight must be lowered. If it shoots too low, the front sight is lowered. It won't take much movement to shift the point of impact by a good bit, so do the cutting only a small amount at a time, shooting the gun after each adjustment until it is sighted in properly. It may take considerable time and effort, but in the end, it will be worth it.

Chapter

Heat Treatment

20

Several components of the finished firearm will require heat treatment, both to harden the parts to prevent battering and undue wear and to increase tensile strength and toughness.

Heat treatment can be defined as a combination of heating and cooling operations applied to a metal or alloy in the solid state to obtain desired conditions or properties.

In carbon steel that has been fully annealed, we would normally find two components (apart from impurities such as phosphorous or sulphur). These components are a chemical compound, iron carbide, in a form metallurgically known as cementite, and the element iron, in a form metallurgically known as ferrite. Cementite is made up of 6.67 percent carbon and 93.33 percent iron. A certain proportion of these two components will be present as a mechanical mixture. This mixture, the amount depending on the carbon content of the steel, consists of alternate layers or bands of ferrite and cementite. When examined under a microscope, it fre-

quently resembles mother of pearl and therefore has the name pearlite. Pearlite contains some 0.85 percent carbon and 99.15 percent iron, not counting impurities. A fully annealed steel containing at least 0.85 percent carbon would consist entirely of pearlite. Such a steel is known as eutectoid steel.

Steel having a carbon content above 0.85 percent (called hypereutectoid steel) has a greater amount of cementite than is required to mix with the ferrite to form pearlite, so both cementite and pearlite are present in the fully annealed state.

When annealed carbon steel is heated above a lower critical point (a temperature in the range of 1325 to 1360 degrees Fahrenheit depending on the carbon content), the alternate bands of ferrite and cementite will begin to flow into each other. This process continues until the pearlite is thoroughly dissolved, forming what is known as austenite.

If the temperature of the steel continues to rise, any excess ferrite or cementite present in addition to the pearlite will begin to dissolve into the austenite until only austenite is present.

The temperature at which the excess ferrite or cementite is completely dissolved in the austenite is called the upper critical point. This temperature has a far wider range, depending on the carbon content, than the lower critical point.

If the carbon steel, which has been heated to a point where it consists entirely of austenite, is cooled slowly, the transformation process which took place during the heating will be reversed. The upper and lower critical points will occur at somewhat lower temperatures than they did during the heating.

Assuming that the steel was originally fully annealed, its structure upon returning to atmospheric temperature after slow cooling will be the same. By "structure" I'm referring to the proportions of ferrite or cementite and pearlite present with no austenite remaining. However, as the steel's cooling rate from an austenitic state is increased, the temperature (at which the austenite begins to change into pearlite) drops more and more below the slow-cooling transformation temperature of approximately 1300 degrees Fahrenheit. As the cooling rate is increased, the laminations of the pearlite, formed by the transformation of the austenite, become finer and finer until they can be no longer detected even under a high-power microscope, while the steel itself increases in hardness and tensile strength.

As the cooling rate is further increased, this transformation suddenly drops to around 500 degrees Fahrenheit or lower, depending on the carbon content. The cooling rate of this sudden drop in transformation temperature is referred to as the critical cooling rate. When a piece of carbon steel is cooled at this rate or faster, a new structure is formed. The austenite is transformed into martensite, which is characterized by an angular needlelike structure and an extreme hardness.

If the steel is subjected to a severe quench or to extremely rapid cooling, a small percentage of the austenite may remain instead of being transformed into martensite. Over a period of time, this remaining austenite will be gradually transformed into martensite even if the steel is not subjected to further heating or cooling. Since martensite has a lower density than austenite, such a change, or "aging" as it is called, often results in an appreciable increase in volume and the setting up of new internal stresses in the steel.

The process of hardening steel consists fundamentally of two steps. The first step is to heat the steel to a temperature usually at least 100 degrees Fahrenheit above its transformation point so that it becomes entirely austenitic in structure. The second step is to quench the steel at a rate faster than the critical rate to produce a martensitic structure.

The critical or transformation point at which pearlite is heated into austenite is also called the decalescence point. If the temperature of the steel was observed as it passed through the decalescence point, you would notice that the steel continues to absorb heat without rising appreciably in temperature, although the immediate surroundings become hotter than the steel.

Similarly, during cooling, the transformation or critical point at which austenite is transformed back into pearlite is called the recalescence point. When this point is reached, the steel will give off heat so that its temperature will momentarily increase instead of continuing to fall.

The recalescence point is lower than the decalescence point by anywhere from 80 to 210 degrees Fahrenheit. The lower of these points does not manifest itself unless the higher one has first been passed completely. These critical points have a direct relation to the hardening of steel. Unless a temperature sufficient to reach the decalescence point is obtained so that the pearlite is changed into austenite, no hardening action can take place. And unless the steel is cooled suddenly before it reaches the recalescence point, thus preventing the changing back from austenite to pearlite, no hardening can take place. The critical points vary for different kinds of steel and must be determined by testing in each case. It is this variation in critical points that makes it necessary to heat different steels to different temperatures when hardening.

After the hardening process, most, if not all, steel parts will require tempering, or drawing. The purpose of this is to reduce the brittleness in the hardened steel and to remove any internal strains caused by the sudden cooling in the quenching bath. The tempering process consists of heating the hardened steel to a certain temperature and then cooling. With the steel in a fully hardened state, its structure is made up mostly of martensite. However, when it is reheated to a temperature of about 300 or 750 degrees Fahrenheit, a tougher and softer structure known as troosite is formed.

If the hardened steel is instead reheated to a temperature between 750 and 1285 degrees Fahrenheit, a structure known as sorbite is formed. This has somewhat less strength than troosite, but it also has considerably greater ductibility.

Actually, what all this boils down to is simply this. Many of the parts that you have made or will make will require hardening. In certain instances this is required only to prevent undue wear, and in others, both to increase strength and to prevent battering or other malformation.

So it will be necessary for you to heat the part to be hardened to a temperature above the upper critical stage (forming austenite), then cooling it rapidly by plunging it into a quenching bath, which may be oil, water, brine, etc. (forming martensite). The hardened steel is then heated once more to a temperature somewhere between 300 and 1290 degrees Fahrenheit and cooled (forming either troosite or sorbite). The exact temperature required for this tempering or drawing operation varies considerably, depending both on the carbon content of the steel and the strength and hardness requirements.

A gas or electric furnace is almost a necessity for this type of heat treatment. If you anticipate treating many parts, I suggest that you either buy a commercial furnace or build one. A usable gas furnace can be built by simply lining a steel or iron shell with firebrick, then adding a vacuum cleaner motor and fan for a blower. A pyrometer is also necessary to measure and regulate the temperature.

It is possible to harden and temper parts by using the flame of an oxy/acetylene torch or a forge or by hot bath. The latter method can be either a chemical solution or molten metal. This method is especially well-suited to irregularly shaped parts, parts with holes, and parts varying in thickness or mass. All these parts will heat uniformly to the desired temperature in a bath.

There are times, however, when the only available method will be the torch. While this method may be far from foolproof, if sufficient care is taken, satisfactory results can be obtained.

In many cases you will not know the exact composition of your steel, so before beginning, a bit of experimenting is in order using a scrap of the same material. Since most of the medium- and high-carbon steels must be heated to between 1400 and 1650 degrees Fahrenheit for hardening, try heating the scrap to a bright, clear, glowing red, devoid of any yellowish tinge. This is the "cherry red" so often mentioned in connection with heat-treating activities. Then plunge it into a quenching bath of water or SAE #10 motor oil, which is at room temperature or slightly warmer. It should now be so hard that a file won't touch it. If it is not, try another scrap at a slightly higher temperature. When the proper combination is found, apply it to the part to be hardened.

Nearly all carbon steels change color in the same way and at almost the same temperature, so the hardening and tempering colors that appear while heating will indicate the approximate temperature of the metal. The chart at the end of this chapter gives a fairly broad color range and can be used as a guide.

There is presently a product on the market called Tempilaq that can take some of the guesswork out of the temperature control. It is available from gunsmith supply houses. A thin coat is applied to the surface of the material to be heat treated. Actually, only a thin smear is required. After it dries to a dull finish, begin heating the metal. When the required temperature is reached, the Tempilaq will melt sharply and should be quenched immediately. Tempilaq is available to indicate temperatures from 350 to 1550 degrees and is the most foolproof temperature indicator I have found except for the expensive pyrometers.

Regardless of the temperature indicator used, the hardened steel must be tempered, or drawn, after quenching. So either wipe on a smear of Tempilaq or heat the metal to the color indicating the temperature desired, then allow it to cool. It would be wise to again experiment with a hardened scrap of the same material before attempting to temper the actual part, and test it again with a file and a punch.

Another method that can be used for drawing at temperatures up to 500 degrees is use of the kitchen oven. Simply place the parts in the oven, set it to the desired temperature, and let it heat for approximately one hour.

Still another method that works well on small parts such as firing pins, sears, and triggers is the use of a hardening compound such as Kasenit. By heating the part to be hardened to a cherry red, dipping it into the hardening compound, reheating to the same cherry red, and quenching in water, a hard surface will result while retaining a soft inner core. This is similar to the case-hardening process, which I will not attempt to describe here since the Kasenit process will give similar results with less equipment.

It might be helpful to include a brief breakdown of the SAE numbers used in drawings and specifications to indicate a certain type of steel. We read about 2340, 4140, 1035, etc., which to the average person mean little or nothing. The first figure indicates the class to which the steel belongs. Thus, 1 indicates a carbon steel, 2 nickel steel, 3 nickel chromium, 4 molybdenum steel, 5 chromium steel, 6 chrome vanadium steel, and so on.

In the case of the alloy steels, the second figure generally indicates the approximate percentage of the alloying element. Usually, the last two figures indicate the average carbon content in hundredths of one percent, or points. Thus 2340 translates to a nickel steel with approximately 3 percent nickel and 0.40 (forty hundredths) of 1 percent carbon.

The color chart at the end of this chapter may come in handy when tempering using the color method. Brightly polish the part to be tempered so that the color will show, and heat it until it reaches the desired color, after which it is allowed to cool slowly.

It should be remembered that the methods and descriptions in this chapter apply to carbon steels only. While the alloy steels discussed may be heat treated similarly, certain alloy steels require entirely different methods of heat treatment.

If the metals described in Chapter 3 are used as recommended, the following heat treatment procedure can be used:

Bolts, barrel extensions, receivers
4130-4140: Harden at 1500-1600 degrees Farenheit, oil quench, draw at 1000 degrees Farenheit.
2340-2350: Harden at 1450-1500 degrees Farenheit, oil quench, draw at 900 degrees Farenheit.
3140-3150: Harden at 1500-1550 degrees Farenheit, oil quench, draw at 900 degrees Farenheit

Sears, Hammers, Triggers, etc.
4140: Harden at 1500-1600 degrees Farenheit, oil quench, draw at 800 degrees Farenheit.
Made from annealed flat spring stock: Harden at 1450-1550 degrees Farenheit, oil quench, draw at 600 degrees Farenheit.

A water quench can be used instead of the oil. However parts are more likely to crack or distort.

Please remember, since I have no control over the methods or quality of materials you have used, I will assume *no* responsiblity for any problems you may encounter in the practices described here.

HARDENING AND TEMPERING COLORS	DEGREES FAHRENHEIT	TEMPILAQ AVAILABLE
Pale Yellow	425	400-413-425
Pale Straw	450	438-450
Yellowish Brown	500	475-488-500
Light Purple	525	525
Purple	530	
Blue	550	550
Dark Blue	600	575-600
Bluish Green	625	650
Barely Visible Red	900	
Blood Red	1200	
Cherry Red	1400	1350-1400-1425
Light Red	1500	1480-1500
Orange	1650	
Yellow	1800	
Light Yellow	2000	
White	2200	

Chapter

Metal Finishing

21

Regardless of what color the final finish is to be, the end result will depend mostly on the quality of the polishing. The very best job will have an even color, all tool and abrasive marks will be removed, and all corners and sharp edges will still be cornered and sharp. Flat surfaces will be flat, without high and low places. When the finished job is held up to the light and sighted along the surface, true straight lines, without ripples or waves, should be evident. Screw and pin holes must not be rounded or dished.

If it is intended that our prototype be shown and offered for sale, we should try to obtain the best finish possible. In many cases an outstanding appearance impresses buyers more than performance. Since we already have outstanding performance, it is imperative that we have a finish to match.

It is possible to obtain an acceptable polish using motor-driven, abrasive-coated buffing wheels if one has sufficient experience with such. However, like many other skills, this requires extensive practice.

The very best polish and finish obtainable to the novice will be obtained using files, progressively finer grades of abrasive cloth, crocus cloth, and finally, if desired, polishing the finished surfaces with the finest grade of white rouge polishing compound on a loose cloth wheel.

Of course it is desirable to have power polishing equipment, mainly as a time-saving measure. Power polishing can result in top quality, but only after extensive experience. The equipment required will include a motor of at least 1 horsepower, preferably with a double end shaft. An arbor is installed on each shaft and a polishing wheel mounted on each of these. Several wheels will be needed—at least one hard felt wheel and several cloth wheels, preferably in an 8 inch diameter. Each of these wheels should be used with only one grit of buffing compound. At least two "loose" or unsewn should be included.

Polishing is done by applying a coarse grit buffing compound to either felt or cloth wheels. This is followed by progressively finer grits on their individual wheels. Felt wheels should be used when polishing over pin or screw holes and on flat surfaces. This is especially true when straight lines and sharp corners are to be maintained. Crosswise polishing should be avoided whenever possible. The parts should be held square to the wheel but at an angle to the floor and polished lengthwise whenever possible.

Hand polishing is accomplished in generally the same manner. Files are used to remove tool marks, dents, etc. Many times it is necessary to draw-file barrels and receivers by grasping each end of the file and pulling or "drawing" it sideways along the length of the work with a steady pressure. If this is properly done on mild steel, it will remove metal in strands much like fine steel wool, leaving a smooth finish. While time consuming, this is one of the very best ways to obtain a uniform, ripple- and wave-free surface, especially on barrels.

This is followed by using strips of abrasive cloth, starting with a fairly coarse grit, in shoe shine fashion, around the curved surfaces of the barrel and receiver alike. This is followed by lengthwise polishing using strips of the same abrasive cloth wrapped around sanding blocks or files. Lateral depressions and circular machine marks will be apparent when this is done.

Continue the process, crosswise followed by lengthwise polishing, until all imperfections are removed. Finally, after careful polishing with the finest grit cloth available, polish all surfaces with crocus cloth. Use the cloth in both directions, but finish with lengthwise strokes as you did with the previous polishing.

If power wheels are available, this can be followed by a careful buffing with the white rouge compound, first on a soft felt wheel, then a sewn cloth wheel. Finish with a loose wheel.

If a dull military-type finish is desired, the white rouge polish should be eliminated. Instead, all exposed surfaces are sand blasted or bead blasted, leaving a dull frosted-appearing surface. This is desirable when a nonglare finish is required.

The polished metal should be examined in bright sunlight to be sure no scratches or polishing marks remain. If satisfactory, the individual parts must be degreased. There are several kinds of grease-cutting compounds and detergents available in grocery and hardware stores that can be used for this. Mix these compounds with water and boil the parts in the solution for a few minutes. After rinsing the parts in clear water, they are ready for the bluing process. Now that the parts are degreased and clean, they should no longer be touched with bare hands but with metal hooks or tied to wires since the oil in the skin of your hands may contaminate them.

The most widely used bluing process at present is the caustic nitrate bath. With this process the parts are polished, cleaned, rinsed, and immersed in a solution that is heated to a temperature of 280 degrees to 350 degrees, depending on the mixture used. After the color develops, the work is rinsed and oiled. Since this process involves less time and is more certain than most other methods, let us look at it first.

A minimum of two tanks are required. Five or six are desirable. These tanks must be long enough to hold the longest barrel and receiver that you expect to process and should measure at least 6 inches wide and 6 inches deep. The tanks should be made from black iron sheet metal, preferably 16 gauge or thicker, and with welded seams. Galvanized or stainless metal should not be used. The galvanizing would soon be eaten away by the bluing salts and would probably ruin the salts in the process. Stainless tanks can cause a galvanic battery-type action between the stainless and the gun steel, using the bluing salts as a conductor. This can result in various colored streaking in the blue job and, sometimes, actual stainless deposits on the gun parts.

Burners must be used to heat at least two of the tanks, preferably three. These are sold by gunsmith supply houses. You can make them yourself using 1-inch pipe of sufficient length to heat the entire length of the tank. Drill two rows of 1/8-inch holes spaced 1 inch apart with 3/4 inch between the rows for the individual gas jets. Cap one end of the pipe and attach a mixing valve to the open end. Mixing valves are available as salvage from discarded gas stoves and heaters.

Either natural gas or bottled gas can be used to fuel the burners. Bottled gas (propane) burns hotter than natural gas and requires smaller jets in the mixing valves. The jets may require drilling out to a larger diameter if natural gas is used or installing a bushing with a smaller hole (or orifice as it is commonly referred to) if propane is used.

An angle iron rack should be made up to

support the tanks. Build it so that the tops of the tanks are at a comfortable level so that parts to be processed can be placed in the tanks and removed without any exaggerated movement on your part. A crosspiece is fastened across each end of the rack some 4 inches below the rack to support the burners.

There are several different brands of commercial bluing salts available from different sources. Regardless of what they may claim, they are all similar. None is so superior to the others as to render them obsolete. Most are similarly priced. Cooking time and temperature will vary somewhat among the different brands, so read and follow the seller's directions carefully.

It is also practical and possible to mix your own bluing salts. One mixture that has worked satisfactorily for me consists of 25 pounds of sodium hydroxide (lye), 12 1/2 pounds of ammonium nitrate, and 2 ounces of trisodium phosphate mixed with 5 gallons of water. The ammonium nitrate is available from feed and seed stores where it is sold for fertilizer. The sodium hydroxide is cheaper if purchased in bulk from a chemical supply house. It is also available in grocery stores in 12-ounce cans, which will cost over three times as much as it will from the chemical supply house. It is also available sometimes at radiator shops, where it is used to clean radiators.

The solution should be mixed either outside or in a well-ventilated room, since a considerable amount of ammonia gas is generated while mixing. Use only a small amount of water to dissolve the other ingredients, since a boiling action may take place while mixing. The remainder of the water is then added.

The solution should be allowed to boil for at least 30 minutes after the initial mixing. The temperature should then be adjusted to between 280 and 295 degrees by adding water if it is too hot, or allowing more to boil away if not hot enough. The parts can now be placed in the tank. They should be suspended using wires or metal rods so that none come in contact with the bottom of the tank.

After 20 to 30 minutes at the suggested temperature, remove the parts from the tank and rinse them in cold water. If the color is satisfactory, boil the parts either in clean hot water or water to which a small amount (2 or 3 ounces

per 5 gallons of water) of chromic acid is added. This is done in an attempt to remove all traces of the bluing salts. If any salts remain in crevices or seams, they will eventually "bloom" out when the weather is damp and humid and form a white powdery scale.

The parts are then dried and oiled, after which they should be hung up and left alone for at least 24 hours before handling or assembling. This is because the blued surfaces tend to get harder and tougher after about a day and will resist scratching or blemishing far better than when they first come out of the tank.

It will be helpful to add a half pound of lye occasionally. It is also a good idea to add between a half gallon and a gallon of water each time after turning off the heat under the tank.

Certain parts will turn red, bronze, or chocolate brown. Usually these parts will take on the same blue black color as the rest of the parts if repolished until bright when they are again placed in the bluing bath before it reaches operating temperature. The parts are left in the bath until enough water boils away for the temperature to rise to 310 to 325 degrees.

The color produced by the ammonium nitrate/lye solution is almost jet black, with a gloss, or sheen, directly proportional to the polish job. A lighter blue color can be obtained, if desired, by substituting sodium nitrate for the ammonium nitrate. This solution, however, is much harder to control than the first one and will not wear nearly as well, so it is probably wise to stick to the ammonium nitrate solution.

It should be mentioned that these solutions will simply eat aluminum as well as lead and soft solders. Therefore, any part made of or containing any of these must be kept out of the tank. Otherwise you probably won't see it again.

Whatever you do, protect your eyes and bare skin from these hot solutions. Water should be added slowly with a long-handled dipper so that you are out of reach of any drops that spatter or pop out. Better still, put a funnel in the end of a 5-foot section of pipe and pour the water through it slowly. You should also avoid breathing the fumes given off when the bath is boiling. Sodium nitrate fumes will lower your blood pressure dangerously, and some commercial salts contain sodium cyanide, which is highly poisonous. So be certain you have adequate ventilation. Always keep in mind that these solutions are dangerous when handled carelessly.

When I was a small boy, the blue considered the best available was the slow-rust method. Many people still consider it so. One such solution consisted of the following mixture:

Tincture of Ferric Chloride	1 oz.
Alcohol	1 oz.
Bichloride of Mercury	1/4 oz.
Nitric Acid	1/4 oz.
Copper Sulfate	1/8 oz.
Distilled water	1 quart

Mix in the order given and store in colored bottles. These should be labeled poison. Let stand for at least 72 hours before using.

This is a slow-rust process requiring some 10 days to produce an adequate finish. When properly applied, it will outwear most other finishes.

Parts to be processed are polished and degreased as previously described. After degreasing, the parts must not be handled by bare hands since oil secreted by the human skin may prevent the bluing solution from working properly. Boil a new pair of cotton gloves and dry them. These should be worn to handle the degreased parts.

Prepare the barrel by making hardwood plugs to fit into each end of it. These plugs should be at least 3/4 inch in diameter and long enough to serve as handles. Turn the plugs a few thousandths larger than the chamber and bore, grease them lightly, and drive them into their respective ends of the barrel.

Most of the other parts can be handled by wooden handles attached to them. Screws and bolts are handled by drilling holes in wood strips and screwing the threaded ends into the holes. Small parts can be handled by the free end of a stiff wire wound around an area of the part that does not require bluing.

To use the solution, swab it on the degreased parts using long, even strokes to give a light, even coat. When coated completely, the parts are placed in a warm, damp place for 10 to 12 hours. The rust that forms during this time is carded off using a small soft-wire brush or fine steel wool. These should also be degreased. The parts are then boiled in clean water and coated again with the bluing solution. This process is repeated every 12 hours for 10 days, after which the parts

are boiled to stop the rusting action and given a coat of oil.

Another popular method in the past was the hot water method. This is still the one to use on double-barrel guns with soft-soldered ribs. Actually it is quite similar to the slow-rust method, but the boiling temperature accelerates the process. While this is referred to as a fast process, it will actually take about two hours. The formula is as follows:

Potassium Nitrate	3/4 oz.
Sodium Nitrate	3/4 oz.
Mercury Bichloride	1/2 oz.
Potassium Chlorate	1/2 oz.
Distilled Water	10 oz.
Sweet Spirits of Niter	1/2 oz.

Put the first four ingredients, which are in powder form, in a colored glass bottle. (In the last few years, potassium chlorate has become considered a controlled substance since it can be an explosive under certain conditions. It is quite likely that you will be required to purchase these four items already mixed from a drug store.) Warm the water and pour it in. Stir with a glass rod until cool. The sweet spirits of niter is then added and the solution allowed to stand for a few days before using.

It should be pointed out that solutions similar to these are available already mixed from various sources. The formulas given are included in the event that you choose to mix your own. Several years ago I included them in another book. Over the years a number of people have written saying that their local drug stores have no knowledge of sweet spirits of niter. Phone calls to five local druggists disclosed that two had it in stock, two offered to order it for me, and the other didn't know what I was talking about. So it is still available.

The parts are prepared in the same way as with the slow-rust method. Again, the cleaned parts must not be touched with the bare hands. The tank is filled half full with clean water. A small wide-mouth jar is fastened with wire in one corner of the tank and a small quantity of the bluing solution poured into it. A clean swab is also placed in the jar. Then the water is brought to a boil and the gun parts immersed in it and allowed to continue to heat until the parts are as hot as boiling water can make them. They are taken out one at a time and swabbed with the warm bluing solution. The parts should have sufficient heat to dry immediately. Each part is then dropped back in the tank and the process repeated on each other part in turn. The parts are then removed, one at a time, and the rust carded off with fine steel wool, then dropped back in the tank for reheating. The entire process is repeated from eight to ten times on each part or until they are blued to your satisfaction. Following this the parts are boiled for several minutes to stop any further rusting action and oiled.

If the operator does his part, this method will result in a finish that is equal in every respect to the caustic nitrate method.

Another method which could be of interest to the occasional bluer is the fuming method. A tank to boil the parts in with a suitable heat source is required, as is a plastic or fiberglass box with a lid that fits close enough to make it as airtight as possible. It should be long enough to contain the barreled action. You will also need a small quantity of both concentrated hydrochloric and nitric acids, and several plastic cups to hold the acids.

The parts are polished and degreased in the same manner as before. Rubber plugs or corks are placed in each end of the barrel. Any surfaces that are not to be blued can be coated with lacquer, varnish, shellac, or similar. The parts are then placed in the plastic box. Several drops of each acid are placed in plastic cups (don't mix them) and two or three cups of each acid put in the box and the cover put in place. The actual bluing takes place in one to three hours. Therefore the work should be examined frequently after the first hour and removed when the desired color is obtained. Making the box lid from clear plastic can be an aid to easy inspection.

When finished, the parts are boiled in clean water to stop any further action and oiled in the same manner as with the other methods. It is possible to achieve almost any degree of luster desired by varying the acid quantities. Since the nitric acid does the actual bluing, while the hydrochloric fumes simply etch the surface, a bit of experimenting is necessary to achieve the desired finish.

There are times when the appearance of the finished firearm can be enhanced through the use of more than one color. Receivers colored with a french grey or case colored can present a striking contrast when combined with a blue barrel and small parts. They will, at least, attract attention.

The grey color can be obtained with the following solution:

Antimony Chloride	1/4 oz. or 120 gr.
Gallic Acid	1/4 oz. or 120 gr.
Ferric Chloride	10 oz. or 4800 gr.
Water	1 gal.

The work is polished (many times finished by light bead blasting) and degreased as usual. It is then immersed in a heated (140 to 160 degree) solution. The first color to appear will be a pale blue. This will pass through several shades of progressively darker blues to purple and finally to grey. If left in the solution long enough, the metal will assume the grey color, but any of the intermediate colors can be produced simply by removing at the desired stage. A bronze color can be obtained by using it cold.

The case-hardening colors can be imparted by, after polishing and cleaning as usual, painting the work with a coating of tincture of benzoin. When dry, an oxy/acetylene flame with a slight oxydizing flame is brought into contact with the work and a small spot or strip is heated until it just changes color. The part is cooled quickly in water to keep the heat from spreading, and an adjacent strip or spot is colored and dunked in the water. The process is repeated until the entire surface is colored. It is important that the metal be quenched as soon as the color appears. If allowed to overheat, the finish will char. Also, be aware that the little single-bottle propane torches are not suitable for this. The area treated must be heated quickly and cooled before the heat is allowed to spread. When finished, the work should be given a coat of lacquer, varnish, or similar to keep the color from fading. Quite vivid color patterns can be obtained with this system.

Chapter

Marketing Your Design

22

Now that you have your design turned into a working prototype—tried, tested, and functional—all that remains is to let the word out that you have such a gun and sit back and wait for the gun companies to outbid each other for the privilege of manufacturing your gun. Right?

Not quite. Most of the existing firearms manufacturers couldn't care less what sort of design you have. If they are making money on what they have in production, they won't want to change. If they are not, they won't spend the money to tool up for a new design.

Perhaps a recap of some of my own experiences are in order. At least you might learn what not to do.

In the late 1970s I had a successful trap gun business. I built release triggers, installed screw-in chokes and adjustable ribs, and built custom trap guns to order.

Then, suddenly, we discovered that my mother had terminal cancer. She had a comfortable home of her own and wouldn't go to a nursing home. So my wife and I took turns looking after her. My wife stayed with her in the daytime, and I stayed at night. This slowed my gun business quite a bit. Then my youngest son got in trouble with the law. Serious trouble. He, together with three others, got drugged and liquored up one night and forced their way into a man's home and robbed him. In the process one of the others shot and killed the man. The state charged all four with capital murder and eventually tried and convicted all four. They are still on death row in the state prison.

Now, in addition to trying to look after my mother, I had to try to help my son too. I had very little time for gun work. My customers started calling and complaining because I wasn't getting their work done fast enough. Finally, after several weeks of trying to do what little I had time for, I had all I could stand. I sent everyone's money back who had paid deposits on custom trap guns, returned all the guns that had been sent to me for conversions, and simply closed my business up.

After almost a year, my mother died. A short time later my son was sent to prison. I needed to get back to work. Of course my trap gun business was gone by now. I have never taken kindly to repeated phone calls from anyone, and I had lost my temper several times with some of my former customers, so I probably couldn't get them back even if I wanted to.

I realize that nothing is gained by losing one's temper. But consider just this one example. The doctor sent my mother to a hospital some 300 miles from home for surgery. I took her there, and since she was all alone, scared and 73 years old, I stayed there with her to offer what comfort I could.

The second night I was there, I was paged to come to the phone. It was a customer of mine from California who had ordered a trap gun.

"Where's my gun?" he demanded.

I asked him how he knew where I was. He said he had called my home and my wife told him.

"Then you know the circumstances of my being here," I said.

He said he wasn't interested in my troubles. He wanted his gun, and he wanted it now.

I told him he would wait until I took my mother home before he got anything from me and hung up the phone.

The next evening he called me again. He said he wasn't satisfied with what I told him the night before. He said he had already paid me a thousand dollars on the gun and he intended to have it. He would tolerate no excuses.

I told him I would go home on the weekend and would send his money back. He said he didn't want his money back. He wanted the gun. I then told him, rather forcefully, that he would wait until I got it finished and hung up.

This still didn't get my message across. He called me again the next night and went over the whole thing again. This time he demanded a delivery date.

I had put up with all I could stand by now. Fortunately I had managed to hold my temper, but this jerk was going to be repaid in kind. I told him I was going home for a day and would put his gun in the mail.

"I knew you could do it if I stayed on you hard enough," he crowed. "I'll expect it next week."

So I went home a couple of days later and boxed up a barrel blank, a piece of tubing for the receiver, three blocks of wood for the stock, grip, and forend, and blanks of steel cut to outline for the small parts. I shipped them to him together with a curt little note advising him that this was all I had at the time and when he could spare them long enough to send them back and I would finish them when I got around to it. I also stated that I did not intend to be harassed in the meantime.

You could almost hear him scream without the telephone. But he got the message this time. In a few days he sent the parts back and left me alone. I screwed him around for almost a year before I finished his gun, just for meanness. I'll never get him back for a customer, but if I had it to do over, I'd do it again.

So I wanted to try something else for awhile. During the time I stayed with my mother I designed a 9mm machine pistol and a box-magazine shotgun. After building prototypes of these guns, I advertised them for sale in *Shotgun News*. To my surprise, here came all sorts of people wanting the design rights to these guns.

First there was a little fat creep from Tucker, Georgia. He claimed to represent the Saudi Arabians and offered me a contract that would have brought me $5 million over a period of time. He didn't have two quarters.

Then there was a guy from Wisconsin. He talked a good game, but he told it different every time we talked. He called me, sometimes twice a day, and described his "small *but honest*" company which he said was devoted to quality above all else. He said his company couldn't pay any money up front, but he would pay a 6 percent royalty on each gun produced and would build a high-quality, top-dollar gun. He mentioned a retail price of $750.

I let him have one of my prototype guns, which he took all over the country. He told me he could sell these guns just as fast as they could be produced, and that he already had orders for 5,000 guns. He wanted a final design differing slightly from the prototype I had already sent him. I set to work building another gun with the changes he wanted made.

During the time I was working on this gun, I received a contract from his attorney which not only would have granted them the right to license others to manufacture my guns, but specified a royalty of 5 percent instead of the 6 he promised.

I immediately sent it back and gave him to understand that we were supposed to have a deal at 6 percent. I also stated that they would not have any right to license others to manufacture the guns unless I agreed to it. I suggested that we forget the whole thing.

As soon as he got the contract back he started calling me. It was just a misunderstanding, he said. I told him I hadn't misunderstood anything. He promised to do one thing, and then changed it, and I wasn't having any. He insisted on sending another contract.

During this same time period he wanted me to make up a compact .22 Magnum pistol. He said it should be no larger than the little .25-caliber pistols already on the market and have a 2-inch barrel. I told him I would see what I could come up with. It didn't take long to determine that such a gun was not feasible. With a 2-inch barrel, there wouldn't be enough slide travel for it to feed shells from the magazine. When he called me again, I told him this. He decided the gun could have a 3-inch barrel but no more and to see what I could do with this.

I agreed to try, and I asked him to send me a letter stating exactly how much I would get, in dollars and cents, as royalties on both the shotgun and this gun.

I dropped him a note the next day stating that the small .22 Magnum pistol simply wouldn't work out. I suggested that we shorten a .30 carbine case and go with a .32 Long or rimless magnum instead.

In a few days I got a letter from him stating that I would get $9 per shotgun and $1 per pistol. He also stated that since he was paying for it, he intended to have the little pistol in .22 Magnum and it was not up to me to change it.

I became enraged at this. Nine dollars is 6 percent of $150, and $1 is 6 percent of $16.67. I wrote him a letter and advised him of this. I don't like telephone conversations when I'm mad. I sometimes say things that I shouldn't under these conditions. I also told him that I had never seen him pay for anything yet and to design his own pistol. I also demanded my prototype shotgun back and informed him that we would have no further dealings.

He called me as soon as he got my letter. Very indignant. He said he would have to hire salesmen to go on the road and sell these guns, buy product liability insurance, discount the guns heavily in order to sell them, and several other things which I no longer remember. But I told him to send my gun back and not bother me anymore. To his credit, he did return my gun.

Then there was a self-proclaimed genius and would-be gun expert here in my home state who insisted that a 9mm conversion unit to mount on an M16/AR15 lower receiver would be a gold mine. Here again, if I would design and build a prototype, he would produce and market the unit. Since he actually owned a manufacturing facility capable of producing these, I agreed to do this. I built a prototype and took it to him. It worked perfectly, and he shot me a line of BS about how they would have it in production in 60 days.

Some three months later, he called me and gave me to understand that the conversion unit wouldn't work. I pointed out that the prototype I turned over to him worked. He agreed that it did, but he said they had changed it some to make it easier to manufacture and the ones they made wouldn't work. I offered to come down there and straighten it out, but the arrogant jackass informed me that he knew more about manufacturing weapons than I did, and it simply couldn't be built. I promptly washed my hands of the whole matter and went on to other things.

Another time, one of this country's leading firearms manufacturers called and asked me to come to their factory and bring one of my shotguns. They said they would pay all of my expenses if I would come. They were interested in buying the rights to the gun, or so they said. I told them I would go to the airport the next morning, and if there was a ticket there for me, I would come. If not, I would go back home.

They called back a couple of hours later and told me they had a flight set up for me early the next morning and what airline to go to. The ticket was there, so I went. One of their people met me at the airport, and after we retrieved my gun, took me to their plant. When we got there I was met by two others who suggested that we have lunch and tour their factory. I agreed, but wondered what to do with my gun.

"Just leave it on the desk there," one of them said. "It will be safe until we get back."

I left it there just like he said. It was in a hard case. I let them take me to lunch, followed by a tour encompassing most of their factory. After some three hours of this, I asked them to take me back and let me show them my gun since I wanted to go back home that same evening. With some apparent reluctance, they took me back.

It didn't actually surprise me all that much to find my gun missing upon our return. When I asked where it was, one of the people said I shouldn't worry, that their people had probably taken it into the next room to look at it. I didn't wait to ask, I simply walked to the door and jerked it open. Sure enough, there was my shotgun. They had taken it apart, and now they didn't know how to get it back together again. I realize now that there was only one of me and eight or nine of them, and I should have kept my mouth shut. But this kind of behavior made me mad. I called them everything I could think of while I was gathering up my gun parts and throwing them in the case. I offered to fight any or all of them.

"Bill, I'm sorry," the ringleader said as I stalked out the door.

"You sure as hell are," I replied, and just kept walking.

I walked down the road to a gas station and called a cab to take me to the airport. Luckily for me I had some money along. I had to pay my own way home.

At just about that same time, several articles appeared in various gun magazines featuring my guns, including at least two on the front cover. In just a short time I had sold all the guns I had on hand. A man in Houston, Texas, called and wanted to know how he could get one of the guns.

"Send a federal firearms license and the money," I told him, "and be prepared to wait at least a week for it. I am sold out and have to make some more."

I put together a gun for him and had it ready when his money came. I shipped it the next day. About a week later he called and wanted to distribute my guns. I told him I could sell all I could build myself and didn't need any distributors. A couple of days later he called again and wanted to know if I would come to Houston and discuss letting them manufacture the guns. Like the others, he promised to pay my expenses. This time I insisted that a round-trip ticket be waiting at the airport when I got there. It was.

These people treated me exactly as I thought they should. I stayed two days with them. They wanted to form a big company to build and market my guns, they said. They showed me three different buildings which they said belonged to them. They promised me a share of the company and $5,000 per month as a consultant fee, or salary. I agreed to this and went on back home.

They called me almost every day, telling me about the progress they were making. Finally, one day they asked if I would let them have a few more guns to show to their investors, or "our" investors, as they put it. I had a few more guns on hand by this time, so I sent them three more.

All of a sudden I quit hearing from them. I tried to call them, only to find their phones had been disconnected. I sent them two certified letters asking for my three guns back. These letters were returned undeliverable. My guns were eventually found in a pawn shop. Some other people that I knew in Houston told me later that these people had gone all over town trying to attract investors. They managed to get a few thousand dollars and promptly left town. No one has seen them since.

Another fellow came into a nearby town and bought a resort and amusement park. He got with me before long and wanted to start a large gun company. He claimed to have $300 million in European banks that he had made dealing in water in Algeria. He said he needed to get his money into this country and invest it. He promised to put $3 million in a company to manufacture my guns.

By now anyone would think I would be wary. But this guy had bankers and lawyers following him around, trying to make sure they got a piece of the action, so I figured he must be legitimate if they all thought so. We executed a contract and he gave his lawyer a check in the amount of $30,000, which was to be put in an escrow account and turned over to me as soon as I delivered six prototype guns. He also gave me a check for $1,500 drawn on the same New Jersey bank as the other check. I advanced him cash for this check.

Here again, I got fooled. But so did several others. Not only did my checks bounce, he gave his own lawyer a $15,000 check for legal work. He gave the resort owner a check for $40,000 as a deposit on the property and some other people a $20,000 check as a deposit on another piece of property. None of these checks were any good. The last I knew he was in jail, but I never got a dime.

All told, I entered into agreements nine times whereby other people would produce my guns. None ever worked. At least three of these times I withdrew because I caught the others lying to me. I think most of the others didn't work because the people I was dealing with couldn't attract investment capital like they thought they could.

I have used several pages here supposedly telling you how to market your design. Instead, all I have succeeded in doing is to prove that I do not have sense enough to market my own designs, let alone yours.

The truth of the matter is, if you contact any of the established gun companies offering a firearm design, they probably won't even answer you. If they do, it will probably be to get you to sign an agreement which says that if they have already thought about a design similar to yours, that they don't have to give you anything for yours. In other words, they can steal it if they like it.

It is difficult, at least, to obtain a patent on a firearm anymore. Almost everything that is currently dreamed up has been done before. I thought I had a new locking system in my inertia-locked shotgun, but subsequent investigation revealed that a similar locking system had been used in 1912. But you should probably go ahead and apply for a patent before you show your design to anyone who might be interested in producing it. This will enable you to at least prove you had it first.

Learn from my mistakes. If you let anyone take any sample guns, insist on being paid for them before they leave your possession.

If you enter into a manufacturing agreement, insist on an advance on your royalties. If they can't pay you anything, they probably can't produce it either.

Don't trust anybody. Greed will make liars and thieves out of an amazing percentage of otherwise honest people if they smell enough money. If the people you are dealing with lie to you, quit them just as soon as you catch them at it. If they will lie once, they will surely do it again.

If you actually have a firearm that is different enough from its contemporaries to stand out, works flawlessly, and can be produced at a price that would be competitive costwise, you should try to attract the attention of some of the gun writers. If they like the gun, they will give it all the publicity you need. You should also display samples at gun shows. If you can afford it, the SHOT show will showcase your design before more manufacturers and dealers than any other single exhibit. You should also advertise in trade papers such as *Shotgun News* and *Gun List*, both of which offer reasonable advertising rates.

With this much exposure, if anyone is interested in producing your design, they will surely manifest themselves. Draw on my experience and don't turn loose what you have until you have an ironclad agreement. Trust only yourself.

Good luck.